SPECTATOR
IN HELL

Colin Rushton

To Annie and George
who gave so much

Acknowledgements

Morris Hatton, Mithras Film Productions for his film, *Satan At His Best.*

The Werner Library for supplying the photographs.

SPECTATOR IN HELL
ISBN 1 901442 06 3

First published in 1998 by Pharaoh Press
Second edition published 1998

Printed in Great Britain.

PROLOGUE

The train ground to a halt and the sliding doors of the carriage were crashed open. The two dozen men inside raised their hands to the sun and in turn jumped down from the train. They were met by a chorus of commands from the handful of Wehrmacht guards awaiting their arrival.

'Bewegen sie! Bewegen! Schnell!'

Falling into some semblance of a formation, the men slowly grew accustomed to the bright daylight after several hours in the dark and took in the scene before them. Their eyes were met by a vision of rural tranquility. To one side, fields of yellow clay rolled into the distance and to the left was a romantic little copse, a perfect retreat for a courting couple.

There were no factories in sight and no building work was in evidence. From where they stood there was no sign of any industry taking place at all. They had crossed the German border the night before and guessed they were probably now in Poland. Discussing their new location quietly among themselves, the consensus of opinion was that they were destined for farmwork. As prison camp work went, this was good news; they would have plenty of fresh air and there should, at least, be an abundance of fresh fruit and vegetables to eat.

Looking down the length of the train, Arthur noticed hundreds of bundles a yard or so from the track. There were trousers, shirts, skirts and shoes, some clearly belonging to young children. Only mildly curious, he thought little of it; he was far too relieved that his worse fears regarding their destination had not been realised.

A short march brought them to a camp and if Arthur felt any apprehension as he entered the gates, it soon disappeared. Inside the perimeter fence were ten wooden huts. The POWs were ushered into the nearest and they were each pleasantly surprised by how dry and clean it was. Further investigation revealed central-heating pipes running the length of the hut, hot and cold running water at each basin and solid bunk-beds, upon which were clean and adequate mattresses.

For the next two weeks the men settled themselves into what they hoped would be their accommodation for the rest of the war and it was anybody's guess how long that would be in the spring of 1943.

A week later, Arthur woke slowly to the noise of guards stomping through the hut's central corridor, crashing rifle-butts on doors. Over the past few days the number of British prisoners in the camp had swollen to nearer two hundred, but they had been required to do little or no work and had been reasonably well fed.

The guards were smiling and enjoying themselves, but there was no friendship in it. There was something sinister happening and they were about to find out what it was.

'Der Feiertag endig! Arbeiten sie jetz!' Those who had more than a smattering of the language were asked what was being said and Arthur learned they were being sent to work. Knowing this moment would come sooner or later, the men shrugged and made their way out to the parade area.

Once gathered into formation, they were marched out of the camp and along a dusty road running through a forest. Arthur, with his mates, was up at the front. On route they came across a group of prisoners working to one side of the road. They were Ukranian women digging ditches under the watchful eye of several armed guards carrying coiled whips. The fear and tension in the women's eyes was tangible. Prior to their arrival the men had been at Farasabrina in Italy and Arthur had drawn the lowest card and missed out on what turned out to be a fairly straight-forward escape bid. He wondered now how much he would soon regret that.

A few minutes later they came upon a factory and to the side of the road was a young girl of about fifteen being severely and brutally flogged with a riding crop by an officer of the SS. Kneeling helplessly in front of him, the young girl was facing the oncoming POWs and presented to them a figure of terror. Her hair had been carelessly shaven and her scalp was cut. Fresh wounds inflicted by the German officer were bleeding and small red rivers ran from her forehead to her chin.

She was naked from the waist and Arthur could see from her ribs and drawn cheeks that she had not been properly fed for some time. The officer momentarily stopped for breath and the young girl looked up. Her eyes were saucepan wide as she pleaded to the sadistic monster before her to relent. He laughed out loud and shouted across to two of the guards standing by. Then he carried on mercilessly whipping her across the head and shoulders.

For some of the Tommies watching it was too much. One of the lads tapped Arthur on the shoulder and stepped forward.

'Come on, lads,' he said, 'I've had enough of this little bastard!' Arthur and three others followed him, walking purposefully towards the SS officer. Arthur shouted for him to leave the girl alone. Unused to such a challenge to his authority, the officer was momentarily taken aback, but as they closed in he took the whip into his left hand and reached for his pistol. At the same time, a soldier of the Wehrmacht raised his rifle and aimed it at the men. The soldier's call stopped them in their tracks.

'Anhalten sie! Er werde getut!' Translation was hardly necessary; if they took another step, the officer would shoot them dead. There was no camaraderie between the two Germans. What the soldier was telling them was for their own good. 'Zuruchgehen sie!' The men stopped and the officer smiled across to the rifle-bearing soldier. Still holding his pistol, he walked towards the Tommies.

As it was Arthur who had shouted out, he stood in front of him and stared coldly into his eyes. The officer was the proto-type of Hitler's Ayrian Adonis: tall, handsome, blond and steely-blue eyed. Arthur dared to stare him out, his own revulsion of the man overcoming the fear he felt. Without dropping his cynical smile, the officer nodded and backed away.

'Ein anderer Zeit,' he whispered to Arthur with menace, 'another time'. Arthur was in no doubt they would meet again before very long. Orders were barked and the men were ordered back into the column. Marching again, they looked behind them and saw their intervention had done the girl no favours. The officer beat her now with a greater ferocity than ever. Arthur clenched his fists and grimaced. He knew her only crime was to be Jewish. She would not live much longer.

Arthur woke with a start, his body trembling and sweating. The nightmare was frightening and familiar. It was one of a number he had endured for nigh on forty years. His wife, Olwen, had long ago become used to his sudden screams in the night. She got up without comment and made her way downstairs to the kitchen. A few minutes later, she came back with a cup of tea and a couple of aspirins, as she always did. She held a vinegar soaked flannel to his forehead and muttered her usual words of comfort.

'Same old nightmare again, love?' Arthur nodded, but this was much more than a nightmare. He was reliving an incident from which he had never mentally recovered. In 1943, Arthur had been captured and sent to a succession of prison-of-war camps before being interned just outside a small Polish town for nearly two years. When the war was over, he had tried to talk about his experiences, but found it very difficult to talk about what he had seen. In any case, he knew that few people would believe him; there were no Tommies there, only Jews.

But Arthur had been there. The camp was near to a beautiful village in Upper Silesia known to the local Poles as Oswiecim. The Germans, though, gave it another name, now synonomous with mankind's most perverse and darkest hours.

They called it Auschwitz.

CHAPTER 1

Arthur Dodd was born and raised in the Castle district of Northwich, a small Cheshire town on the River Weaver. His mother's first husband had been killed in the trenches of France during the First World War and had married his father, a regular soldier in the Cheshire Regiment, just after Armistice Day. Arthur himself arrived on 7th December, 1919.

His father was an austere, distant man. He had served in the Boer war at the turn of the century and as a sergeant had been captured during the Great War. As a parent, he was distinctly military and Victorian in his attitude and had little time for Arthur and his younger sister.

At fifteen, Arthur left school and was taken on as an apprentice mechanic at Northwich Transport Company. There he learned to drive and began to understand the mechanics of the internal combustion engine under the watchful, friendly eye of his boss, Harold Isherwood. For his labours he was paid all of ten shillings (50p) a week, but Arthur had already taken the first steps down the path that would lead him to Auschwitz.

The company owned a Ford People's Popular saloon car, which was used to transport mechanics to broken-down lorries. Arthur fell in love with it the first time he saw it. It was in this car he had been taught to drive and, having added a year to his age when completing the driving licence application form, he passed his test in the early part of 1935. A year later, he repeated the lie and passed his HGV test.

Those early working days were fun for Arthur. Harold took to the young man and they would often go fishing together in one of the many meres in the Cheshire countryside. Arthur had to serve under the Articles of Apprenticeship for seven years, but when Harold opened his own transport company in 1937, he invited Arthur to finish his time with him.

Tempted though he was, ten shillings a week was hardly conducive to living away from home and Arthur had to decline. His mother, too, was against it, as she was against the transport business in general. In those days a driver had to find his own consignments and could be away from home for as long as three weeks at a time.

In Harold's absence, Arthur quickly became bored and began looking for another company to take him on. When he was eighteen he entered the world of scrap, being employed as a driver by Jimmy Caffrey, a well respected, local entrepreneur. Caffrey only had the one vehicle and most of the work was sub-contracted from the Middlewich Borough Council. Consequently, Arthur was home every night by tea-time and was paid the quite princely sum of £5 a week.

Caffrey was a decent man and would often make his lorry available transporting local people to Clatterbridge Hospital on the Wirral. For this extra work, he paid Arthur five shillings, half of what he had earned at the Northwich Transport Company for a full week. For many, Caffrey's lorry was the only way they could get to the hospital to visit sick relatives, but he never objected to those who jumped aboard for the day out.

'Take your mum along,' he used to say to Arthur, 'the run will do her good. 'Despite his generosity and kindness, Mrs Dodd was still unhappy about the driving her son had to do and finally persuaded him to join the Weaver Navigation Company. His grandfather had sailed on the Salt Union boats and his Uncle Jack was a foreman there. To please his mother, Arthur had to give up his beloved driving and also take a serious cut in wages. At the WNC he started on just one guinea (£1. 05) a week, rising to thirty-eight shillings (£1. 90) when he was twenty-one.

He gave most of his wages to his mother, as he had done when he worked for Caffrey, so in fact it was she who suffered as much as anyone with his loss of income. She was, though, more concerned with his long term prospects and saw security and advancement in his new position.

For three months, he was employed over at Weston Point, Runcorn, where the building of a number of clay sheds was being completed. He had to ride the thirteen miles to work each day on an old 'sit-up-an-beg' lady's bicycle and when the wind was against him the journey could take as long as an hour-and-a-half. Adults were allowed ninepence (4p) a day for travel expenses, but Arthur, under twenty-one, received only sixpence (2 1/2p). As the return fare was ninepence, the road between Runcorn and Northwich was busy with young lads peddling their way to work and back.

In 1938, developments in Germany began to look ominous and talk of another war was in the air. Hitler had been in power for five years and in March Germany had annexed Austria. Ned Bebbington, a huge man, was a good mate of Arthur's at the WNC and during the summer had decided to join the Territorial Army. Arthur was encouraged to do the same, but his mother's response was an emphatic 'no'. Frightened by the ever-increasing probability of war, she knew the territorials would be the first to be called up and wanted her one and only precious son at home for as long as possible. As it happened, Ned became a sergeant with the Cheshires and spent the entire war as an officers' mess manager in Northern Ireland!

It was towards the end of the summer when Arthur was walking two girls along the riverbank near Hartford, in the company of his close friend, Alan Parks.

'I'm joining the navy, Arthur,' Alan told him, 'why don't you join up with me?' Alan was caught up in the patriotic fervour sweeping the country, but Arthur, just short of his twentieth birthday, still needed his mother's permission and once again it was refused. The war was to be a sad time for the Parks' family with both Alan and his brother, George, being killed. Alan lost his life aboard the HMS Repulse in Singapore, while George was shot down serving in the RAF.

In the September, the governments of both France and Britain were seen by many to be weak in their stand against the growing demands and incursions of Nazi Germany. Hitler won a major concession when allowed to seize the Sudetenland, the Germanic quarter of Czechoslovakia, without resistance.

In the same month, it seemed that any possibility of Arthur taking an active part in any war that might break out had disappeared. He was at work and helping to run a boat along its launch ramp when his left foot became trapped between the ramp and a turning wheel. It was some moments before his situation was realised by other members of the working party, by which time his foot was near severed and attached to his leg only by the sinews of his instep. His Achilles tendon was severed and his heel severely crushed.

His foot was saved from amputation and stitched back together by a Dr Booth at the Northwich Infirmary, but he was bluntly told as he endured a slow and painful recovery that he would spend the rest of his life with a club foot. Each day he suffered a course of painful physiotherapy to stretch the Achilles and allow him to put his heel fully on the ground. At times, the pain was unbearable, but in just six weeks he was fit enough to hobble back in to work on light duties as a stocktaker in the company stores.

During the summer of 1939, and despite the efforts of government appeasers, Britain was dragged inextricably towards war. Finally, on September 1st, the German army and the Luftwaffe invaded Poland in a ruthless and murderous blitzkrieg. There was no room left for negotiation. Hitler was ready for a European war and had thrown the gauntlet down. With nervous trepidation, Britain picked it up.

For Arthur, the first few months of war were a huge disappointment, but this was overtaken by grief in February, 1940 when his mother died. She had contracted the influenza bug sweeping the country that winter and died of pleurisy. The lynchpin of the family was gone, but she had departed this world sound in the knowledge that Arthur would take no active part in the war.

Throughout this time, with Dr Booth's assistance, Arthur's treatment continued. They had never conceded that Arthur's injuries were permanent. The press was full of the country's urgent need for volunteers and Arthur broached the subject that he might try and join up. The doctor certainly knew that he had no chance of passing a full medical, but believed it was important that Arthur's mental attitude should remain positive.

'It might be a bit soon, Arthur, to be honest,' he told him, 'but why not go along and see. A country can ask no more of its young men than that they are willing. ' At the medical, he was examined by an orthopaedic specialist, a Dr Hay, who watched Arthur carefully as he stripped down to his underpants and walked nervously about the room. Dr Hay made his assessment and handed the report to the recruitment officer, a veteran of the First World War who wore a scarlet sash across his barrel chest and was the proud owner of a bushy, grey moustache. He looked over the results of Arthur's medical and slowly shook his head.

'I'm sorry lad,' he said, 'but we can't take you. You've been assessed as a B2 and I'm afraid that's not good enough.' Seeing Arthur's obvious distress, he vainly tried to reassure him. 'Look, lad, this is not a permanent grade. Why don't you keep working at it and have another go in a year or two.' Arthur looked at the floor and nodded in silence before turning away. He was about to pass through the exit door when the officer called after him. 'Hang on a minute, have you got a driving licence?' He was obviously doing all he could to accommodate Arthur. Arthur replied that he had a HGV licence and the officer's face brightened.

'Well, lad, I don't know if we can give you a rifle, but you might come in handy as a driving instructor.' He told him that the army would be in touch soon. Arthur was lifted beyond words. At least, he thought, I'll be in uniform and doing my bit. He smiled to himself when he thought of his mother. He would be in the army and back behind a steering wheel. She would have had a fit!

'Don't worry, Mum, 'he said to himself, 'I'll be a long way from the fighting. '

CHAPTER 2

The army drivers' centre was located in Foundry Street in Whittington Moor, near Chesterfield and there were approximately 150 men billeted there. Corporal Saxby of the East Lancashire Regiment was in charge of the drill sessions, Colonel Cope was the technical advisor of mechanics and Sergeant Edwards was the weapons instructor. With Arthur as driving instructors were three retired London bus drivers, one of whom was a Sergeant Picket.

The vehicles used for instruction were three-ton Albion lorries with gate-change gears, but when the tuition started on the first morning, Arthur was instructed to line up with the other trainees. He was then crammed with half-a-dozen other men into one of the Albion cabs as each took it in turn to receive instruction. The session was fraught with danger. Most of the lads had never before driven a motor car, let alone a commercial transport vehicle, and how nobody was killed was a mystery for which Arthur thanked the Lord at the end of the day.

When it was his turn, it was obvious that Arthur knew exactly what he was doing. Sergeant Picket gave him a long, hard look.

'What can you drive?' he asked him.

'Anything,' Arthur replied, 'I thought I was coming here to instruct not be instructed!' The error was quickly rectified and later when Arthur was talking to Picket, the old man revealed that he had, in fact, been sent to the school to teach young officers to drive staff cars. For the purpose, the army had provided an old Humber Snipe, but Picket told a startled Arthur that he had only ever been taught to drive a bus.

'You're pulling my leg!' Arthur laughed.

'I'm afraid not,' Picket answered, 'I was taught to drive on a London bus and I've never had the chance to drive anything else. I wouldn't know where to start. '

'Literally, I suppose,' joked Arthur. The thought of getting behind the wheel of a Snipe had always been pure fantasy for Arthur, so he was quick to seize the opportunity. 'Tell you what, why don't I teach you? If you can drive a bus, you'll pick up how to drive a car in no time. While you're getting the hang of it, I'll teach the officers to drive the Humber.' The two became firm friends.

The men were drilled each day and although Arthur was excused physical training, he joined in whenever he could to maintain the programme of exercise recommended by Dr Booth before he left. The war and the idea of impending danger was never very far away from the thoughts of the trainees at the school and soon they would be taking their newly-acquired skills to the front lines around the world, supplying arms and carrying despatches. For Arthur, though, no such fears or excitement troubled him. His war, he thought, would be spent in the Peak District.

There were many laughs amid the tension endured by men about to go to war. On one occasion, a trainee driver by the name of Wilson sneezed on the parade ground and blew his false teeth across the cinder-laden ground. Colonel Saxby had been in a foul mood all morning, but even he had to laugh.

'I know you are all impatient to get at the Germans,' he said, addressing the men generally, 'but it seems that Wilson here would like to get his teeth into them straight away!' The company fell apart at Wilson's toothless grin as he chased after his dentures.

There were many different forms of entertainment at Whittington, not least of which were the regular visits from the local British Legion club of a blind man who was the local draughts champion. He took on, and beat, anybody who fancied their chances as long as they first made a donation to the club's funds.

After a month or so, Picket was rushed into hospital with severe stomach pains and within a few days had died of peritonitis. He had become a close friend in a short time and it hit Arthur hard. There were, though, dreadful things happening all over Europe and he had to put it behind him.

At the outbreak of the war, there was a national shortage of qualified drivers. Only six of the men sent to Whittington had ever driven before and fewer again had been at the wheel of a lorry. Consequently, Arthur's skill was much sought after. It was brought to his attention that the army was asking for volunteer lorry drivers to go to France and help the British Expeditionary Force who were struggling to keep a foothold on the European mainland. The war was going badly and the army was being pushed into the English Channel by the Wehrmacht's Panzer divisions.

Germany had seized both Norway and Denmark in the April and a month later the British prime minister, Neville Chamberlain, had resigned. For some time, Chamberlain had committed his government to a policy of averting war and having failed so completely, was left with little choice but to stand down. A coalition government was formed and Winston Churchill became Prime Minister, but the situation in France did not improve. Belgium was invaded and by the end of May, 1940, many believed that an invasion of the south-coast of England was both inevitable and imminent. They were dark days.

The absolute priority at that time for the War Office was to rescue as much of the BEF as was humanly possible. A huge flotilla of small seafaring craft bobbed across the channel in a seemingly endless roll, bringing back as many men as they could carry. On the French coast, the situation was desperate. In order to assist an orderly retreat, the army needed drivers and Arthur volunteered to go. In such a time of crisis, his incapacity was almost irrelevant.

Late one evening, he was taken south and lodged in a large textile warehouse where he stayed for two nights. He did not have the remotest idea where he was. He was joined there by others from various units stationed around the country and the surface calm belied the nervous apprehension in everyone's heart. There was little or no news coming back from the continent and they were almost totally dependent on rumour and heresay. Such was the tension on the second night that one man lost his nerve completely and began to discharge his rifle. Three men were shot, one of whom died. The broken man was finally overcome and led away, but the incident had done nothing to calm already fraying nerves, especially when word came through that they would be leaving within a few hours.

They travelled by train to the coast, an agonising journey taking more than two days. They were shunted from one siding to another as more volunteers joined the ranks or trains with greater priority were allowed to pass through. Late in the afternoon of the second day, the train arrived at a dockside which Arthur assumed without ever having it proven to him was Southampton. He boarded a ferry and found himself in the company of men from a number of different regiments: Royal Artillery, Royal Engineers and several regiments of infantry. Arthur, on his own, chatted to many of them, but he never again met any of the men with whom he shared that trip.

They were disembarked onto a deserted beach at St Valery-en-Caux, eighteen miles west of Dieppe, with guns of battle clearly audible in the near distance. The men in his company, without an officer present, waded onto the shore, but once they were there they had no idea what they were supposed to do or where they were supposed to report.

They were finally approached by a sergeant carrying a clipboard under his arm who was attempting to impose some semblance of order.

'Can anyone here ride a motorbike?' he asked, clearly much hassled and distraught. When Arthur answered in the affirmative, he got the impression it was the first piece of good news the man had heard for days. With his feet still wet from the water, Arthur was recruited on the spot as a despatch rider.

The bike in question was a suspect-looking 350cc Ariel with its front headlamp hanging off. The sergeant handed him a despatch and pointed him along the coast road for his destination. When Arthur started the bike up, he found it contained low-grade fuel, had a dirty tank and an almost constantly blocked carburettor. He pushed it as much as he rode it.

The simple system of communication being applied was one of a series of despatch riders working in relays along the line of the coast. Consequently, Arthur would ride, or push, the bike along until he met a rider coming the other way. They would trade despatches and turn around. The same system was operating right along the two-mile strip of French territory still held by the British. Working his way along the coast, Arthur ran across the battered remnants of the 51st Highland Division, dishevelled, weary and a desperate shadow of the force they had presented on landing. They had been strafed by the Luftwaffe and pummelled by Rommel's 7th Division. Their broken ranks meandered slowly towards the coast in search of some respite.

He was flagged down by one of their officers searching for some information, but there was nothing Arthur could tell him; he had no orders regarding their position. He was able to tell Arthur that after landing on the French coast they had fought a tenacious and valiant rearguard action for several weeks, but their days were numbered. Arthur left them as he had found them and thought to himself it was well the people at home were not witness to the scene. They would not have slept.

As the days passed, the sound of shellfire grew closer. It would not be long now before Rommell had forced the British army into the sea. The air of inevitable defeat hung heavily over the men, tormented in their retreat by the deadly, terrifying raids of screaming Stuka divebombers, unloading their deadly cargoes of anti-personnel bombs. Among the sand dunes of the St Valery beaches, soldiers were maimed or killed by the lateral-exploding shrapnel that whipped across their lines.

As the noise of each of the bombers faded into the distance, it was replaced by the agonising screams of seriously wounded or dying men. Arthur lost count of the number of times he threw himself from his bike into a ditch as another Stuka bore down on his position. Just when it seemed that they could take no more, the German infantry appeared on the clifftops and began to send down accurate shellfire from their artillery support. When all was lost, the small ships and boats arrived and the men were ordered to swim for their lives. The date was June 11th, more than a week since the beaches of Dunkirk had been cleared.

Understandably, many of the men swam for the nearest boat, but being a strong swimmer, Arthur made for a salvage tug some 500 yards from the beach. He thought there would be less panic further out and less chance of the boat being hit. He swam through the thick oil covering the sea's surface and when he finally made it to the tug, the tyres around the hull were covered in it. Each time he lifted himself clear of the water, he lost his grip and fell back in. He tried frantically, again and again, but he was never close to pulling himself aboard. Finally, almost passing out with exhaustion, he thought of his mother and prepared to meet his maker.

'Won't be long now, Mum, won't be long now,' He slipped below the water and truly saw his life passing before him. Myriad images from his past seemed to flash through his mind: his parents, his sister, the vicar of the Holy Trinity church, Harold Isherwood, Jimmy Caffrey, school mates, the members of the church choir, the man in the fishing tackle shop. Each memory seemed to be restored for his last consideration. As his life ebbed away, he felt himself raised to the surface for what was surely the last time.

And then...and then a new sensation. Suddenly, he was pulled by the hair and raised out of the water. Looking up through oil-filled eyes, he thought he could see a short, stocky man in a woollen hat. The vision seemed ludicrous, but this strange man seemed grimly determined not to lose the precarious purchase he had on Arthur's head. He was unable to lift him onto the boat, but as he hung half in, half out of the water, Arthur felt no pain. He dangled, neither saved nor drowned. Then another face appeared and a strong arm came under his armpit and lifted him up the side of the ship, over the rail and onto the deck. Immediately, he threw up and watched in a daze as his vomit, black from the oil, ran down his legs. Then he passed out.

CHAPTER 3

Arthur was landed at Ramsgate and recovered quickly. Apart from swallowing large quantities of oily water, he had not been hurt. He did spend an unpleasant day and a half constantly vomiting, but following a good night's sleep he was really none the worse for his exertions.

After a medical examination, Arthur joined up with a man named Perkins and the pair were sent to Overstrand, near Cromer on the East Anglian coast. There they joined up with a Home Guard unit, drilling with brush handles and manning a Lewis gun without ammunition. Until 1935, the Lewis had been the standard light machine-gun of the British army, but had since been replaced by the more versatile Bren gun. The army's surplus guns had been distributed to, among others, the Home Guard. When loaded it was capable of firing 550 . 303 bore shots a minute, but in its present state was little more than decoration. The purpose was to give the impression to German surveillance aircraft that Britain was ready and waiting for an invasion, but, of course, nothing was further from the truth.

After the miracle of the evacuations, Britain's position in the war did not improve. By the end of June, the Germans were in Paris and the French had thrown in the towel. Diplomatic relations with Britain were broken off, but the reality was that France had not recovered from the dreadful losses two decades earlier when more than three million Frenchman were killed on French soil. France was not mentally, economically or militarily ready for another war and Hitler knew it. Though Churchill and his ministers continued to lobby the American government for financial aid and supplies, Britain would have to defend her shores alone.

Arthur and Perkins had been at Overstrand only a couple of days when the first reconnaissance Heinkel flew over. The German airplane flew down the coast on a level just below the clifftops and was so close that Arthur could clearly see the pilot's grinning face. Arthur was not sure what annoyed him the most, the German's arrogance or the inability to take a pop at him. As the Heinkel circled around and flew directly overhead, both Arthur and Perkins threw themselves to the ground, memories of St Valery still frighteningly fresh in

Arthur's mind. Instead of firing, the pilot gave them a superior wave and the aircraft disappeared.

Arthur spent only a couple of weeks in East Anglia before he was transferred to Perth, where he became a member of the RASC 'B' Company (Ammunition) and, by coincidence, was attached to the 51st Highland Division. As a driver-mechanic, he looked after the division's commandeered lorries, which included Albions, Morris Commercials, Ford Surreys and a Ford Sussex. The division was transferred first to Grandtown-on-Spey, near the naval base at Lossiemouth, and then to Kinbrace, way up in the Sutherland highlands about fifty miles south-west of John O'Groats. There they took delivery of thirty brand-new three-ton Bedfords.

Since a great number of the 51st had been killed or captured in France, their numbers had been considerably supplemented by new conscripts, most of whom were Glaswegian lads. For a while, Arthur found them impossible to understand and he became the butt of their humour, which escaped him. Slowly, as he began to interpret their dialect he found them to be a sound bunch who would do anything for you.

He shared a tent with three of them, two of whom were brothers. Charlie and Andy were from the notorious Gorbals district of Glasgow and they each carried bike chains and had razor blades stitched into their coat lapels. For the purpose for which it was made, Arthur had a Rolls razor, a gift from his sister, which had rusted badly after his dip in the channel.

'Och, mon!' exclaimed Charlie, 'yiv no need tae poot up with that! Send it tae the makers and tell em what happened tae yae. 'This he did and a short while later he was rewarded with a brand new model that was the envy of the company. One day the razor disappeared at the same time Andy had gone on leave for the weekend. Charlie followed the next day on a twenty-four hour pass and came back without Andy, but with the razor. Charlie had found his brother trying to sell the razor in a pub and beat him up. If the retribution was excessive, he nevertheless demonstrated some awareness of right from wrong.

During the August of that year, the nation held its collective breath as the Battle of Britain took place in the sky over Kent. The newspapers published the daily figures of aircraft being shot down and Arthur felt that even if they were exaggerated, it was obvious the RAF was giving the Luftwaffe a bloody nose. On August 15th alone, the papers reported the loss of nearly two hundred Stukkas. Arthur wondered how many of those Stukka pilots had been responsible for the raids on the stranded troops on the French coast and was satisfied that particular score was being settled.

With Goering's Luftwaffe repelled, an invasion had been temporarily averted and both Churchill and the media milked it for all it was worth. But nobody was in any doubt that the war was far from over.

In North Africa, British troops had driven the Italians across the Libyan border and this first major success of the land forces was encouraging after the debacle in France. In the spring of 1941, attention was drawn to events in the Atlantic and the activities of the German battleship Bismark. The HMS Hood was sunk and a great sea chase and battle ensued before the Bismark herself was finally sunk.

At the same time, orders were issued for volunteers for Africa and Arthur was keen to get involved. Initially, he was rejected but as the urgency for more men increased, the same medical officer who three weeks earlier had failed

Arthur, allowed him to go as long as he was not on active service.

He was put on board the SS Duchess of Athol and set sail from the port of Glasgow's King George V dock. Within a day, he was back on the quayside as the ship returned with a damaged turbine and had eventually left aboard the P & O liner, Stratheden, bound for Port Said.

On their arrival, Arthur was encamped at Genifa and was a regular visitor to the temporary place of worship erected there in the form of a marquee. One Sunday morning, he was alone with the padre at the chapel entrance when they heard the unmistakable noise of a Wellington bomber in trouble. They looked up and watched helplessly as the aircraft circled briefly before dropping out of the sky. They were at the scene of the crash within minutes, but there was nothing to be done. The crew and five passengers were dead and their charred and bloated bodies were laid out alongside the stricken aircraft.

From Genifa, Arthur was moved onto the base supply depot (BSD) at El Kirche and shortly afterwards given orders to relieve the BSD at Tobruk. Due to his experience as a driver-mechanic, normal procedures were overcome in the field and Arthur's captain had his medical status raised to 'A2' category. Simultaneously, his colonel ordered him to drive to a recovery shed some distance away to have some damaged cases repaired. When he got back, the men had left for Tobruk, but Arthur was consoled by now being recognised as being on 'active' service.

News of the war around the globe filtered through to the men in Africa, the most sensational being shortly before Christmas when more than two thousand Americans were killed by Japanese bombers on the Hawaiin US navy base of Pearl Harbour. The Americans were now in the war and that, at least, was good news. A few months earlier the threat of an imminent invasion of England appeared to have been lifted when Hitler dramatically directed his forces east and invaded the Soviet Union. By September, they had reached Leningrad (St Petersburg) and were laying siege to the city. The following February, Singapore fell and much of the news in the early part of the year centred around the Pacific war between the US and the Japanese.

Back at Genifa, life was pretty good, given the circumstances. The men could swim in the 'Blue

Lagoon', as the Mediterranean was called, and discipline was relaxed. Watching a new batch of arrivals, Arthur spotted a man sporting a moustache which gave him an appearance uncannily like Jack Hughes, a good friend from Northwich. That is exactly who it turned out to be and it was good to see someone from home. The two men shared a tent and had a lot to talk about. The company was shortly afterwards joined by an arrogant lance-corporal who had those with nothing better to do picking up waste-paper from all corners of the camp. Nobody was sorry to see the back of him when he was transferred.

A few days later, everyone was posted to Ikingee in Egypt where they joined up with 307 Company (Ammunition) and were attached to the 66th RASC, the largest of its kind in Africa. On arrival, practically the first person they came across was the arrogant lance-corporal from Genifa, now wearing his sergeant's stripes.

Once the full compliment arrived, the company was moved up to Gambut, near Tobruk, stopping en route at Fort Caputso. They had been allocated fifteen old Morris commercials, but the thirty company drivers were taken in two lorries to the vehicle depot at Mena, where they picked up thirty new three-ton four-wheel-drive

Chevrolets on the American lease/lend system. Each truck had two fifteen-gallon tanks with fifteen two-gallon cans strung on a frame under the dashboard. They were faced with a laborious fuelling operation and straws were drawn to determine the order in which the men would be allocated fuel. Arthur drew the short straw so was at the end of the queue, so while he waited Jack emptied his allocation into both his and Arthur's two-gallon cans. This meant that when Arthur had finally been supplied, they had the much simpler task of pouring fuel into the larger fifteen-gallon tanks and a lot of time was saved. The rest of the day was their own and they both set off to see the pyramids.

The following morning, they set off back to Fort Caputso, but after only a couple of miles, Arthur's truck was sputtering and an examination revealed a carburettor full of water. The cans used to fill his tanks had contained water and he was delayed for two days while it was drained. they stayed at Fort Caputso for a fortnight and both Arthur and Jack made the most of the time available to have a look around. The area had earlier in the war been the scene of a battle and the two friends rooted among the debris to see what they could find.

They came across a case of two-dozen cans of bully beef, which they buried in case they ever came back that way and were short of food. Arthur found a German Opal half track and removed the carburettor which he later fitted to the Chevrolet. Although Opal used the same thread as its American counterpart, it had a larger bore and as a consequence Arthur's fuel consumption rose from twenty-five to eight miles per gallon. It was, though, probably now the fastest truck in the desert, a fact that would save Arthur's life before he was much older.

CHAPTER 4

Moving up towards Tobruk, the role of Arthur's company was to supply ammunition to the tanks of the 7th Armoured Division, now being pushed relentlessly back by Rommell's Afrika Korps. The RASC's day of reckoning came on June 5th, 1942, when they were moved up to the battlefield at what seemed the totally inappropriate name of Knightsbridge.

Much of the battle took place in what could be described as an elongated saucer, its raised edges giving the location the look of a football stadium. The battle commanders and the men of the RASC were perched on the saucer's rim and watched a one-sided battle unfold beneath them. The six-pound shells of the German Tiger tanks had a greater trajectory than the two-pound shells of the British Matilda, Valentine and Honey tanks and it made grim viewing.

The battle lasted for just two hours and Arthur was near to tears as it came to a bloody climax. Brave men clambered from their machines screaming, their clothes alight, their tanks were no match for those of the enemy. He had seen dozens of US Sherman Grant tanks on view at Mena, but saw only two this day.

During the battle, the British tanks would raise a grey flag when their ammunition was exhausted and quickly retire to as safe a haven as they could find. On seeing the flag, an RASC truck would be ordered in to meet up with it and replenish its supply. Arthur had been in once, but towards the end of the battle, with the British tanks severely depleted in number, Arthur's turn came again.

A spent tank was told by a captain of the Royal Artillery to hold its position and not seek shelter. Three RASC trucks had been despatched back to the depot for more ammunition and Arthur was behind the wheel of one of the only two trucks still loaded. Despite the stricken tank coming under heavy fire, the captain ordered Arthur into the battle.

Scared witless, he had no choice but to obey the command. 'Well, Mother,' he said to himself, 'I guess this is active service. Look after me.' With his foot almost flat to the floor, Arthur's truck roared towards the tank. He pulled up alongside and almost immediately a Tiger shell went directly through his canopy, missing by inches the loaded shell she carried, but reducing the back of the canvassed truck to its skeletal frame.

Moments later, Arthur was surrounded by a scene of absolute chaos and panic. Defeat had been acknowledged and the captain had given the order to abandon the area. Two Indian gun-carriages swept passed him, their occupants waving frantically at Arthur to get the hell out of it. The captain disappeared and Arthur, now with a corporal for company, made to follow him.

Suddenly, a Tiger came into view on the left and moved parallel to them, just twenty yards away. As the turret was trained in their direction, Arthur turned sharply to the right and drove for all he was worth. He expected to be blown to pieces at any second, but the 'souped-up' engine saved his life. As the Tiger receded into the distance behind him, Arthur thanked the Lord for Opal carburettors.

Darkness descended and a lot of time was lost by the fleeing convoy as they searched for the road to Fort Caputso. Once found, they were diverted by a Red Caps road block and told to pick up what remained of the South Welsh Borderers and an Indian division on the Axis road. They passed a deserted NAAFI building stocked with cigarettes, drinks and chocolate. Fearing the supplies would be captured by the advancing enemy, the captain ordered the stores to be loaded onto the trucks. It was a costly mistake.

The weary troops were not picked up until half-one in the morning and finally they made their way towards safety. An hour later, they were ambushed and the enemy had chosen the site of the attack carefully. As they entered a short horseshoe in the road, the attack broke out and it was immediately obvious there was no escape. A flare lit up the area as if it was the middle of the afternoon and the Germans let them have everything. Everyone scrambled from the vehicles in an effort to escape. Snatching up his valise, Arthur ran for the scrub and threw himself flat to the floor as tracer fire came ripping towards him. The sand kicked up inches from his face and he could hear the bullets whistling just above his head. The scrub offered absolutely no protection at all and it was clear to Arthur that he would be killed in a matter of a few seconds.

Arthur had thought he was about to die once before, when near-drowned off the coast at St Valery, but he had not then experienced the sheer stark terror he felt now. Once again, vivid pictures of his home and family flashed through his mind. Almost ridiculously, he thought of people and events he had not remembered for years. Faces came to him to him to which he could not put names. He recalled incidents from when he was a young child. Finally, he saw his mother. He would be with her soon.

A few yards away, a British officer led a company from the Indian division into an attack on a machine-gun post. Screaming at them in their own tongue, the officer charged forward and was bravely followed by his men. They were cut down before they had covered twenty yards. Arthur had never before witnessed such foolhardy, insane courage.

Whether or not it was brought about by this act of reckless daring, Arthur would never know, but suddenly there was a lull in the firing. Arthur did not think twice. He scrambled to his feet and ran clear of the road, diving into a slit trench some thirty yards away. He stopped for just a few seconds to catch his breath and calm his nerves before scrambling away and heading for the coast road. He did not slow down to look back. Reaching some rocky outcrops, he began walking in the general direction of Egypt. The first battle of Tobruk was over.

Before long, Arthur came across another 'stray' who had managed to escape from the ambush. Back home, the man had been a marathon runner with the Nottingham Harriers, but he had damaged his foot in escaping and it was all he could do to walk at all. Arthur stayed with him, helping him along, making the best progress they could.

During the day, they sheltered from the sun and from the sight of German convoys and patrols. The valise Arthur had pulled from his van turned out not to be his own but that of the corporal who had jumped aboard. Inside was a bible and that was to prove to be a precious crutch in the ordeals ahead of him.

They walked every night, on one occasion coming across a band of Bedouins from whom they were able to buy a dozen bantam eggs. After two weeks, they came across the town of Bardiyah, on the border with Egypt, some sixty miles from where they had been ambushed.

Despite his training, the runner was suffering badly from foot blisters, but as Arthur was exhausted from helping his friend, he volunteered to take a closer look at the town. He was gone for an age and Arthur was relieved beyond words when he finally came back in the early hours of the morning. The town, he said, was crawling with Germans.

When the day broke, they made their way down into a wadi, a dried-up stream containing a number of rocks behind which they could take cover. As they approached it, six German soldiers appeared from behind one of the rocks and confronted them with their rifles pointing directly at them. One of them spoke English.

'Good morning, gentlemen,' he said, smiling, 'we have been watching you for some time.' They were escorted into Bardiyah and placed with thousands of other British POWs already there. Before long, they learned that Tobruk had fallen on June 21st and something like 30,000 Allied troops had been captured. They were made to strip and bathe in the sea and for Arthur, despite the disappointment of being caught, it was the freshest he had felt for some considerable time.

In the water, Arthur was approached by a Welsh lad who suggested they escape by swimming out to sea and into the next bay. The task was a daunting one, but Arthur was confident in his ability to swim the distance and readily agreed. They had advanced no more than twenty yards when they came under fire. The bullets came perilously close and they both immediately stood with their arms raised. As they waded back, they were surrounded by a large number of their compatriots so it was impossible for the German guards to identify the two who had made a bid for freedom.

The following day, they were taken to As-Sallum, some twenty-odd miles away across the border. They were held in an enormous valley, ideal for the purpose of securing thousands of prisoners. German guns were mounted on the high ground and trained on the captives. It was here they were addressed by Rommell, the 'Desert Fox' himself, standing in the back of his car. He spoke to them in five different languages and was asked by one of the men how many he spoke.

'Thirteen,' he replied. Raising his head, he talked as loud as he could, addressing as many of those gathered as were close enough to hear him. 'You have battled bravely for your country, gentlemen, but the fight is over for you now. You will be taken to Germany for the duration of the war. Does anybody have any questions?'

'Food!' shouted several dozen of those standing in front of him. The travelling German food kitchens were excellent and the men, as Rommell promised, were well fed on rice and gherkins. The following day they set out on a 300-mile trek back into Libya to Benghazi, a major port on the Mediterranean's Gulf of Sirte. Most of the men carried their greatcoats, which if an almost intolerable encumbrance during the scorching heat of the day, were an absolute necessity to keep out the freezing cold of the nights.

The long line of Allied prisoners, stretching as far as the eye could see, was an awesome but depressing sight. The passage of humiliation lasted the best part of three weeks and by the time they arrived at Benghazi a great number of men had collapsed and been left behind in the desert. They entered the town in the middle of a thunderstorm and were bedded down for the night among the gravestones of the town's cemetery.

They stayed at Benghazi for two days, but rather than being despatched to Germany as they had been told, they were handed over to their Axis allies and put aboard ships bound for the Italian port of Brindisi, on the Strait of Otranto on the Adriatic coast. The men, many of whom were suffering from a variety of tropical illnesses including dysentery, were put onto two filthy grey coasters. Their South African and Indian allies were boarded onto an older an even more dilapidated rusty-coloured ship. They were crammed like sardines and had to urinate where they stood.

Within an hour of departing, there was an almighty explosion and total panic broke out as each man fought to climb the two steel ladders that led from the hold to the deck. Those unfortunate enough to reach the top of the ladders were immediately battered back down into the hold by the rifle-butt of an Italian guard. News passed down that the explosion had been the ship carrying the South Africans and the Indians, hit by torpedo. All hands aboard went down with her and no attempt was made to pick up survivors. Sitting trapped in the bowels of a ship with a deadly submarine in the vicinity was a severe test of already strained nerves, but the danger passed.

Dropping anchor half-a-mile from the quayside at Brindisi, the men were ferried in flat-bottomed, overcrowded barges into the port. Arthur saw several men being pushed needlessly and cruelly into the sea. The screams of those unable to swim the short distance to the shore was ignored and several men died. Despite the fact that Arthur had now seen action in two theatres of war, it was the first time he had witnessed an example of needless cruelty.

From Brindisi they were transported to Capua, about three-hundred miles away, close to the Mediterranean and about twenty miles north of Naples. They slept on wooden bunks covered in bugs and were fed on just a small piece of cheese and a slice of bread each day.

After two weeks in Capua, they were moved another hundred miles north to Farasabrina, near Rome. 4,000 POWs were encamped in large marquees, each holding a hundred men. Despite the morale of the British soldiers being very low, they still managed to have some fun each morning at the expense of their Italian guards. When the roll call was taken, men would hide and then reappear again for the recount. Consequently, the guards were never able to count the same number twice and the process took hours.

They were fed on one ladle of soup and occasionally a bun. On the rare occasions they saw Red Cross food parcels, as many as ten men had to share one package. They would then use the boxes to catch sparrows to supplement their meagre diet.

A Corporal Guscot, who Arthur had known for some time, approached Arthur as someone who could be trusted to take part in an escape bid. The plan allowed for three of the four men involved to escape and cards were drawn to see who would have to stay behind. Arthur drew a two and it was he who had to stand down. The three men were hidden in tea chests brought in with Canadian food parcels and it was Arthur's job to keep a lookout. The three chests were carried off and after the war, Arthur met up with one of the escapees in Hastings. 'Ginger', as he knew him, was able to tell him that once clear of the camp, they made their way to a small fishing port close to Rome and posed as fishermen aboard a trawler bound for the Greek islands. From there, home was an easy run and the three were each awarded an Oak leaf for their endeavours, a medal which Arthur was denied on the draw of a card. His misfortune, though, was to have far greater consequences.

Arthur spent six months at Farasabrina, after which time, in the early part of 1943, the men were split up and sent to different more permanent camps. Each was asked on an official form to put down their working skills and Arthur had listed 'cat-burglar'. When the groups were made up, he found his sarcasm had landed him with another two dozen jokers who had given the form similar scant respect. They would travel to their new camp, wherever that would be, together.

The first leg of the journey took them to Florence, 150 miles to the north and was a stark contrast to Farasabrina. Here the British prisoners were well regimented and discipline was well maintained. Morning assemblies passed without incident and it seemed to the arriving 'rebels' that the men here had accepted their fate. They were part of Wavel's original army and had been imprisoned for the best part of two years. Their policy of 'no disruption' appeared to work as standards of food and hygiene were high for a prison camp. The new arrivals stuck to their principles of 'no co-operation' during their stopover at Florence. For them, the war was not over.

From there they crossed the border into Austria bound for Innsbruck. The twenty-five 'rebels' were housed in the same rail carriage and an escape plan began to formulate. The boards of the carriage floor were rotten and easily broken up. The idea was to wait until the train slowed on one of the many uphill sections of the journey and, one by one, drop through the hole and wait for the train to pass over.

The plan was foiled when the men of the next carriage set fire to some straw. On arrival at Innsbruck, the carriages were all searched and the hole discovered. As it happened, it was extremely unlikely the plan would have succeeded. When the men were taken from the train and placed where they could be watched, and beaten, they noted a heavy guard presence on the roof of the train. They would have been easily spotted.

The train left without them and the miscreants were sent to a nearby stone quarry where they suffered a week of hard labour at the hands of the SS. Their penance served, they were put back onto a train and sent on to Lamsdorf, a huge transit camp for POWs. Here, new arrivals were deloused and had their heads shaved. They were also photographed and given their POW numbers. For Arthur, that number was 221925, stamped on both halves of a metal disc, perforated through the centre.

From here, some were sent to the graphite mines in Austria and others to farms and factories. The troublesome twenty-five of Arthur's party were sent to a coalmine in Poznan and as with most units, Arthur's group contained its 'barrack-room lawyer'. It was he who had instigated the ill-fated escape bid from the train and he had kept a low profile since their visit to the quarry. Now, he was finding his feet again.

'The Geneva Convention strictly forbids forcing POWs to help the enemy's war effort!' he told them. 'Working in a coalmine constitutes just that! We will not go down that mine!' Their refusal to work led to them being severely beaten with rifle-butts and jackboots. It also meant, after being completely starved for twenty-four hours, another transfer.

In the east, the Germans had lost half-a-million men in the freezing cold of the Soviet winter and in North Africa the British Eighth Army had taken Tripoli and Tunis. By the beginning of May, 1943, the war in North Africa was won. Since the outbreak of war, many things had happened to Arthur to lead him to this moment, but the dye was now set. What followed over the next two years would live with him forever. Early one morning, the 'rebels' were once again crammed into a train-carriage and taken south. Twenty-four hours later they had travelled two hundred miles to a small town thirty miles west of Krakow. Had they been told the name of their destination, it would have meant nothing to them.

The world was still to hear all about Auschwitz.

CHAPTER 5

The central area of Auschwitz KD Concentration Camp) was divided into three sections: Camp One was the men's prison and contained Jews, communists and other 'undesirables'; Camp Two, to the east, was Birkenau, named after the small village flattened by the Germans when the camp was being constructed and was the women's camp and where the gas chambers and the crematoria were located; and Camp Three, the smallest and known as Monowitz, in which Arthur and the other British POWs were interred.

Around this accommodation were thirty-nine labour camps where prisoners would work in a variety of industrial plants, producing arms, machine parts and chemicals, or in the mines, farms and plantations surrounding the camp. In all, the entire complex was spread over an area of some twenty-five square miles and, according to evidence given at the Nuremberg trials, held as many as 140,000 prisoners at any one time. Arthur was put to work constructing the Buna plant for the manufacture of benzene and synthetic rubber. Any thoughts of refusing to work had quickly disappeared. There was nowhere else to go after Auschwitz; if you did not co-operate here, you were shot.

Each building, made of red brick, had its identity number painted on each gable end and the part of the Buna plant in which Arthur worked was BAU 38. There was a vast range of thirty-five storage huts in a compound, oddly known as Canada, where the clothes and personal belongings Arthur had seen by the railside would have been sorted. Nothing was wasted here; clothing, footwear, brushes, combs, suitcases, spectacles, toothbrushes and even false teeth all had their own storage area. Jewish prisoners who arrived with gold fillings had those extracted, the contents adding to the countless fortunes of the Nazi regime.

The different camps were each surrounded by a triple row of barbed wire supported by concrete pylons. High voltage electricity flowed through the wire and along its length, at intervals of about forty yards, were towers from which guards manning machine-guns and powerful searchlights would monitor the prisoners below.

Behind these imposing fortifications, leading German industrial companies had built their factories and IG Farben, Krupps, Siemens and Schukert were among the well-known names occupying the labour camp areas. Unionwerke, a subsidiary of Krupps, had an explosives factory there. After the war, IG Farben & Co were revealed to have been the manufacturer of the Zyclon gas used to exterminate the Jews. The company maintained Zyclon had been produced only as a disinfectant, but it was classified as Geheimmittel (confidential) and its key elements were chlorine, nitrogen and cyanide. There were, in fact, two types of Zyclon, carried in identical containers: Type A was a disinfectant, but Type B was used in the gas chambers. What was particularly distressing for the British prisoners at Auschwitz was to see that many of the boilers in the camp had been provided by Babcock & Wilcox, a UK company.

For Arthur, the going had been very tough since his capture at Bardiyah. On arrival at Auschwitz, they had marched just two hundred yards to the warm and pleasant huts of Camp E711 in which they spent their first fortnight. They had been purpose-built, they later discovered, for the Hitler Youth and had given them a totally false impression of what awaited them. When they were first installed in E711, their barrack-room lawyer had taken most of the credit.

'Farming is better than mining,' he had told them, 'it shows it pays to stick up for your rights.' When they left the camp a fortnight later and encountered the Jewish girl being beaten by the roadside, the sense of foreboding felt by them all was a far more accurate indicator of what was to come. Their 'lawyer' had been quiet since.

On their first day at the Buna factory they had been divided into working groups, each led by a German civilian and escorted by a German guard. Once organised, they were taken to their place of work. All around them, there were buildings under construction and there was an abundance of SS guards watching those prisoners in blue and grey overalls bearing the Star of David. Occasionally, the men would see a Jewish prisoner laying dead on the floor. Later, a cart being hauled along by other Jews would pick up the dead and take them away.

What especially chilled Arthur and his friends during these proceedings was the apparent distorted normality of it all. Nobody fought back or said a word in protest. It seemed the Jewish prisoners were resigned to their fate. Even when they had nothing to lose, they submitted to this barbaric, inhuman treatment.

Arthur's group were taken to a large enclosure alongside a railway line. Inside were housed long bogie-wagons loaded with pipes of varying lengths and diameters. They were put to work unloading the wagons, being told that this enclosure was to be the technical store for most of the equipment to be used in the factory.

It was like a huge ironmonger's shop, containing valves, tools, timber and neatly stacked bags of cement. Arthur passed the day in a trance, carrying out the tasks set him in a robotic silence. He had witnessed much in the past three years, but he was not prepared for the events that now began to unfold before him.

At midday, the POWs were each given a bowl of soup and a small piece of black bread, made from wild chestnuts and sprinkled in what looked and tasted like sawdust. From what the men could see, the Jews appeared to be barely fed at all, to which their emaciated frames testified. Contact between themselves and the Jews was not permitted. In the vicinity of Arthur's group they were involved in the building of stores and offices. They could be seen mixing cement, laying bricks and transporting various building materials in wheelbarrows.

Each Jewish gang was watched by one of the Kamaradschafts Polizei, known as a kapo, who would kick and beat the Jews around the head with baseball-bat like truncheons if they were slow in their work and sometimes even if they were not. Other kapos carried whips. Arthur could not comprehend the insanity of the place when he noticed that many of the kapos, largely drawn from the criminal elements of the camp, also wore the Star of David. They were, of course, closely monitored and any kapo who would not harass the Jewish prisoners with the enthusiasm and venom of an SS officer would quickly find himself relieved of his position. Seeing one Jew treat another in this way was good sport for the SS.

The working day was finished at five o'clock and they were marched back to Camp E711. They each struggled to come to terms with the events of the day and there was little conversation between them. As they lay in their bunks that night, few of them could sleep, the silence broken only by occasional sobbing. The thought occurred to Arthur, even at this very early stage, that he and his friends had to die here. He could not believe that the SS would allow them to live and tell the tale of what they had been witness to. He lay quietly thinking of home and was sure he would never see it again.

The next two weeks passed in much the same way. Although they watched daily the treatment of the Jews, the only physical injuries incurred by the British prisoners were fractured bones due to a serious calcium deficiency in their diet. From the second day, the good food at the hut stopped and they received little more than potato soup and black bread. They were, to some degree, consoled by the adequacy of their accommodation, but at the beginning of the third week, they were moved.

Their new home was at Camp E715 in the section known as Monowitz, much closer to the synthetic rubber plant and previously occupied by Russian prisoners. They had been worked to death except for the last resilient eighty-odd who were gassed to make way for the more technically competent British POWs. This information had been obtained from a Polish inmate who told them how he had watched as the remaining Russians had been driven like cattle into one of the underground air raid shelters. The downward-sloping ramps had been closed off at either end with steel doors bolted from the outside. The air vents were then fed with Zyclon B tablets, as were used in the gas chambers in Birkenau, and the accommodation problem was solved.

The senior Wehrmacht officer on the Monowitz site was Feldwebel Messer, the equivalent in rank to a sergeant-major. He was, as were all the German officers, a meticulously smart man in his thirties and, from Arthur's experience, fair and even-handed. When they were transferred to his charge, he took the opportunity to split up the twenty-five British troublemakers. The lads, taking consolation wherever and from whatever they could, accepted this as a compliment to their generally uncooperative and disruptive ways. They were each accommodated in twenty-five different huts and assigned to twenty-five different working parties. Even by the almost non-existent standards of hygiene at Auschwitz, Camp E715 was a filthy hole. The solitary latrine was a nine-foot cube dug into the ground right outside Arthur's hut. Across it was a wooden plank and around it a sheet of corrugated-iron for some degree of privacy. Despite their endeavours to debug the huts, they were constantly louse-ridden.

His first meal in the new accommodation was fish that Arthur assumed had once been herring. It stank and he refused to eat it, sure that he would regret it later if he allowed himself just one mouthful. . Those who tried it were sick almost immediately. Fortunately, Red Cross food parcels were still getting through to the men and without them not one would have survived for very long.

The Jews were daily being beaten, gassed and cremated. For many of them, death was a merciful relief, but the constant smell of scorched hair and burning flesh was nauseating and one that Arthur and his fellow prisoners were never able to get used to. The huge red-brick chimneys, tapering towards the top, towered over two-storey buildings and were visible from most parts of the camp. Only a change of wind direction gave them any kind of release from the horrifying smell and was a constant reminder of the atrocities taking place around them. Most Jews were gassed within an hour of arriving at the camp, their ashes dumped in the Vistula river, the largest of the three rivers in the vicinity of the camp.

For a while, Arthur was employed digging ditches and laying pipe for a new synthetic rubber plant. Then he was set to pipe-bending with Charlie Piddock, an arc-welder with Metro Vicks before the war. Their gang consisted of two young Polish lads, three Ukrainian female welders in their teens and a Mongolian girl-labourer. One of the Poles was a handsome, decent man by the name of Stacha, but the other was known as a falsch Deutsch, or 'phoney German', a nasty type who had sold out to the Germans, acting as a spy and an informer. To some degree, Stacha was tarred with the same brush and so nothing was spoken of in their presence. Both Poles were from the nearby town of Oswiecim and did little work. It was safest to assume they were there to monitor any sabotage attempts by the British POWs.

The German foreman, a workaholic who paid great attention to detail, usually had two Wehrmacht guards in attendance. They spent their day in the work's cabin where the group took their midday 'soup'. There were also frequent visits from the SS who would crack their whips against their jackboots and scream at the kapos to extract more work from the Jews. If one did not push hard enough, his armband would be torn from him and he would sent back to work. Once a man had his kapo status removed, he would be entirely friendless in the camp and few survived long.

It was impossible for Arthur to begin to calculate how many Jews disappeared, but there were thousands more from all over eastern Europe arriving every day and they never appeared to swell the population of the camp. The trains pulled in and the chimneys of the crematoria continued to blow its deathly smoke into the sky. For the British observers of this grotesque scenario, they had no need to worry about life or death, or whether they were destined for heaven or hell when their time came. Their time was now and they were in hell already.

CHAPTER 6

There were two currencies in Auschwitz, the lager (or 'camp') mark and barter, the latter of which was by far the most widely used. Guards and labourers who came into the camp from the town were bribed to bring in commodities otherwise unavailable. Red Cross food parcels, though, were the main source of bartering medium. The most sought after goods were soap, coffee, cigarettes, chocolate and clothing. It was the system of bartering that gave the prisoners something to live for.

Due to both its scarcity and the risk in carrying it, clothing was the most valuable commodity and here the artillerymen and engineers had a distinct advantage. Both received regular supplies from their own associations and Arthur was often envious of the goods they received. Arthur himself only ever received one clothing parcel at Auschwitz, and that was so battered and torn it contained just a shirt, a towel and a sock. Sent by his sister, it did, however, contain a Peterson pipe with a silver ferrel. Pipe tobacco was impossible to purchase in the camp and in order to derive as much pleasure as he could from it, he would meticulously dry out whatever spent tea leaves he could find.

Some temporary release was offered by alcohol. The only drink available was loosely termed 'schnapps', but in truth was methanol. It was a lethal concoction and those who resorted to it were sent crazy before succumbing to a slow and painful death. There were notices all over the camp giving warning of its toxicity, but where there is need there will be trade and some of the hardest men sought solace and a permanent escape in this way.

Arthur earned three lager marks a week, but they could buy precious little in the camp and nothing at all outside. The cheap paper bore the legend lagergeld, the mandatory eagle symbol and a number indicating its value. From the camp could be bought a grey, sudless soap, dubious looking cigarettes, ersatz coffee and razor blades. The Germans were curiously keen for the prisoners to shave and Arthur always it assumed it was for the purpose of propaganda photographs. Arthur and his friends would shave regularly but refused to have their photograph taken.

Making a stand against the wishes of the German authorities had little effect on anything but the men's morale. A Corporal Jim Purdy was in charge of Arthur's hut and he consistently paid great attention to the men's state of mind. It affected everybody on the occasions when one of the lads broke down. One of the Welsh Borderers became increasingly unstable and began to bare his chest to the Wehrmacht and SS guards, taunting them as they raised their rifles to him.

'Shoot me!' he used to shout, 'go on, shoot me!' The guards got to know him well and he was a regular source of amusement to them. They would push him around with their rifle-butts in the confident and arrogant manner of those convinced of the invincibility of the Third Reich.

Alan Blades was a young lad from East Dereham in Norfolk, tall and slim and the wearer of stainless-steel rimmed glasses. Unlike the Welshman, Alan mumbled to himself and escaped the horrors about him into a world of his own. He'd been captured at Dunkirk at the beginning of the war and had suffered severe hardship over a prolonged period of time. More and more, he had withdrawn into himself.

Jim Purdy did everything he could to look after the man's interests. As the officer in charge of a group of men, Jim was not required to work each day and kept Alan on light duties. In this way, he could keep an eye on him during the day and Arthur would do the same of a night. Only 4% absenteeism was allowed at any one time, regardless of the general health of the men, and it spoke volumes for the moral-fibre of Alan's comrades that not one soldier voiced a word against the special treatment given him.

Another prisoner of E715 was a tall, agile man, known to his comrades to be a religious maniac. He was a devout follower of God's word, but saw every issue in black and white and, consequently, argued that every German person, man, woman and child, should be wiped off the face of the earth. He would rant this message into the faces of the guards and he came perilously close on many occasions to being shot dead where he stood.

There were varying degrees of mental instability among the men and it showed itself in different ways. One night, as they were trying to sleep, one man rose from his bunk, left the hut and walked straight over to the wire. He had but one thing on his mind and that was to quietly crawl under the wire and leave. Everyone heard the shouting and the gunshots. When the full story emerged the following morning, it seemed he had given the guards a run for their money. When the shooting started, he had fled to the ablutions block and hidden in its attic. There he stayed until the guards burst through the door and sprayed the ceiling with machine-gun fire. The appearance of blood dripping to the floor let them know they had found their target.

An unexpected source of anxiety and distress often came in the form of letters from home. It was unlikely that wives and girlfriends had any idea of the trouble their missives sometimes caused, but many times they were enough to send a man over the edge. A woman's written words could do more damage than anything encountered at the camp.

There were several illiterate prisoners in Arthur's section and frequently he would read their mail for them. On one occasion, he was approached by the youngest of them, waving a recently received precious letter from home. They retired to a quiet corner of the hut and Arthur slowly read its contents to a man who had married not long before he was called up. At the end of the first paragraph, Arthur stopped abruptly. The man's wife had given birth when her husband had been away for what was now the best part of three years. Arthur had to think quickly. What should he do? He pretended he was struggling with the handwriting when in fact he struggled with the dilemma before him. Should he tell the truth or should he omit the offending news and temporarily spare the man's feelings? Obviously, the poor lad would be able to do nothing but stew in his heartache.

Whether he was right or wrong, Arthur could not decide, but he wanted to be no part of anything the man might do to himself as a consequence of hearing this news. He left out the details of the birth and read the letter through as if everything at home was fine. He handed the letter back.

'Thanks, Arthur,' he said, 'you can read the next one she sends me,' but Arthur doubted if there would be any more.

The British POWs took great risks in getting what scraps of food they could to their fellow prisoners in the Jewish section. However, as the British and American air forces began a sustained bombing campaign of German cities, so deliveries of Red Cross food parcels became more scarce and it was all they could do to keep themselves alive. Arthur thought back to the time he had spent at Farasabrina and how they had used boxes to catch sparrows. He put the idea to a few of the lads and they spent the next few days searching for birds to capture. In all that time, they did not see one bird in the vicinity of Auschwitz. Whether it was the smell of burning flesh, the smoke of the crematorium or a natural sixth sense that kept the birds away, Arthur did not know. He can, though, testify that there were no birds about Auschwitz in the time he was there.

Arthur was kept busy with the building of BAU 38, bending pipes and making gaskets and their German foreman was keen to keep them at their work at all times. Although Arthur remained convinced he would never see home again, he continued to look for ways to sabotage German operations whenever he could. He forced stones into pipes, fitted blank flanges, always aware of the need to have eyes in the back of his head. As everyone was on the verge of starvation, one piece of information from an informer might be rewarded by additional rations and it was impossible to know who could be trusted. Arthur saw himself as a doomed man who might, even in the most insignificant way, do something to upset the Nazi war machine before he lost his life. The slightest interference for which he was responsible gave him enormous satisfaction.

The war carried on and it was news of it that usually brought the most cheer. The Italians had unconditionally surrendered by the end of September, 1943, and the Russians were beginning to squeeze the Germans from the east, retaking Kiev at the start of November. Although it was not revealed to the world until after the war, it was at this time that Heinrich Himmler made his now infamous speech declaring his plan for 'the extermination of the Jews' and 'a never-to-be-written page of glory'.

Arthur had spent the previous Christmas in the relative comfort of Farasabrina, but the festivities in Auschwitz towards the end of 1943 were muted and depressing. For Arthur, his life was over. Only his pride, self-esteem and a bloody-minded determination to hang on kept him going. He was unaware that events around Europe were turning against Hitler and his fanatics. The Allies were pushing back the German war machine, but it would be a long time yet before Arthur would see any light at the end of the darkest of tunnels.

CHAPTER 7

During the bitterly cold weeks of January, 1944, Arthur's group was joined by a 'gang' of Jews controlled by a particularly vicious kapo, determined not to lose his privileges. They were building an internal wall for the new BAU 38 plant and had set up a cement mixer alongside the fire burning outside. Arthur's attention was attracted by the physical condition of one of the Jewish prisoners. The man sidled over towards the fire to steal a few moments of warmth, only to be chased by the kapo within a minute. Seeing his condition, Arthur thought one good blow from the kapo would probably kill him.

He carried bricks on a hod from the pile outside to the site of the wall inside, staggering under the weight of each load. He wore only a flimsy pair of shoes with the soles dangling off and he wore no socks. Arthur decided to find a pair of socks for the man as soon as he could. He had recently received a small parcel from his step-brother, Franklin, and was able to trade twenty cigarettes for a new pair of woollen socks owned by a soldier of the Royal Engineers. The following day, he concealed the socks inside his jacket and looked for an opportunity to slip the socks to the man.

He was poised to make his move when from the corner of his eye he saw the SS officer he had first encountered beating the Jewish girl a couple of weeks after his arrival. He was the epitome of Teutonic arrogance and strode towards Arthur, cracking his whip against the leather of his boots. Arthur froze. He picked up a pipe and pretended he was checking the angle of the bend. The officer walked passed him but continued to watch the area for another ten minutes. Eventually, he left and Arthur was able to pass the socks on. The man smiled warmly at him and revealed a mouth of blackened or missing teeth.

The following morning, Arthur noticed the man was not wearing the socks and he quickly rounded on him.

'Where are they? 'he demanded, pointing to the man's feet. He could speak no English, but knew well enough what Arthur was talking about. He pointed to his mouth and Arthur understood too. The man had traded the socks for food. Two weeks later, he did not show up for work one morning and Arthur never saw him again. He did not need to ask what had happened.

There was only ever, at the most, four hundred British soldiers in Auschwitz at any given time and as the Germans strictly applied the maximum permitted sickness of 4%, there never more than sixteen men 'allowed' to be sick. There were two British medical officers in the camp, Captain Spencer and Captain McFarland, and two orderlies working in the Krankenhaus, or hospital, outside of which there were always long queues of men wishing to be considered as being sick.

Arthur had spent two weeks in the camp hospital having lost his voice and running a temperature. The symptoms were not unlike those for typhus, rampant at Birkenau and in the male sector of the Jewish camp. Arthur was treated by Captain Spencer, Captain McFarlane and a German doctor by the name of Schmidt, who drew from him a yellow substance during a very painful lumbar puncture. After further blood tests, Arthur was diagnosed as having pneumonia, but he would never have pulled through without the constant care and attention of Captain Spencer who watched over him, mopping his brow every night for a week.

Among the Polish labourers who lived in Oswiecim and worked each day in the camp were a number of Partizans who risked their lives as a matter of course to hinder Nazi operations. Once in your trust, they would die for you, but they took swift retribution against any man or woman who betrayed them. Arthur was approached by one of them, who indicated he had been told Arthur could be trusted. He offered to smuggle in radio parts in exchange for cigarettes and chocolate. Arthur was very interested.

Rumour had been circulating in the camp that increasingly the war was turning against Germany, but it was impossible to know what was and was not true. The positive effect that such confirmed news would have on the morale of the prisoners was incalculable. Arthur took the man up on his offer. Two nights later, Arthur received the precious parts and made his way back to the entrance of E715. To his horror, he saw that everyone was being thoroughly searched and among those present was the SS officer he had encountered earlier. This man had made a point of randomly searching Arthur whenever the opportunity arose, but to date had found nothing.

For Arthur, this sudden decision to search everyone was too much of a coincidence. He wondered if the young Pole had been threatened in a bid to set Arthur up. Perhaps their earlier conversation had been observed by suspicious eyes. Arthur's mind was full of the possibilities, but what really mattered was if he could avoid the very serious situation he now found himself in. There was nobody he could pass the equipment to and he could not drop it anywhere on the open, barren ground. Instead, he had no choice but to have the incriminating evidence found, much to the smug satisfaction of the SS oficer.

He was marched from the camp and through several other compounds by the officer and two SS guards before coming to the road that led to the main entrance to the camp. Arthur walked under that now infamous entrance bearing the ominous warning over the gate.

'ARBEIT MACHT FREI'

The principle of 'freedom through work' was one close to the Nazi heart, especially when applied to the hundreds of thousands of Jewish prisoners in Auschwitz. The brutal reality for those people was that death was the only path to freedom. For himself, Arthur had no idea what to expect. He was now squarely in the Jewish quarter of the camp and he knew of no other British soldier who had been to this part before him. Certainly, nobody had lived to tell the tale. He had, though, heard enough rumours of red-hot pokers and the extraction of finger nails to give him cause for the gravest concern.

He was pushed roughly through the doorway of a large room inside which was a senior officer of the SS seated behind a desk.

'Mr Dodd, is it?' he said, with excessive politeness and an almost Oxford-English accent. 'Take a seat.' Arthur's palms were damp with fear as he sat down before this imposing man. 'You will appreciate that we do not have time to waste, so I will come straight to the point. I have just one simple question for you and I require from you one equally simple answer, after which you will be returned to your quarters. Who gave you the wireless parts?' Arthur hesitated before answering.

'The whole thing was a set-up. You know exactly who gave me the parts.' Arthur did not feel the indifference he tried to convey. A thin, condescending smile spread across the officer's lips, but Arthur's answer was ignored and the question was repeated. Arthur gave the same reply.

'Please, Mr Dodd, do not underestimate the gravity of this situation. Think very carefully before you answer again. From whom did you receive the wireless parts?' Arthur looked directly into the man's eyes and was under no illusions. He was in very serious trouble.

'You already know,' he insisted. The officer's smile disappeared in an instant and he nodded curtly to the guards standing behind Arthur. He was hit across the back of the head by a rifle-butt and sent crashing to the floor. There, he was kicked mercilessly by the SS officer and the two guards and although Arthur covered his head and rolled into a ball, he could not escape the blows. There was a momentary pause while he was asked the question again. The same answer brought another flurry of kicks and blows.

Arthur was about to pass out when he was dragged to his feet and taken from the room. Another door was opened and he was thrown into a darkened, windowless cell. He lay on the damp floor, finding breathing both difficult and painful. He had a vague feeling he was not alone in the room, but soon fell into a fitful, troubled sleep.

He was awoken by the door being flung open and as he was dragged to his feet he seriously doubted his ability to withstand much more punishment. The light from the doorway revealed his cell mate to be the camp leader, the British officer responsible for the POWs by the name of Innes, whose battered, swollen face made it almost impossible to recognise him. Arthur wondered how long it would be before his own physical condition was the same.

He was marched outside and taken towards the main gate. Looking to one side, he saw three Jewish prisoners still strung up after being hanged from a wooden scaffold. As bad as he felt, this chilling sight shook Arthur to his roots. He was pushed forward, but instead of passing under the main gates was led through a different part of the camp. They turned away from the Jewish sector and passed only SS guards and their vicious snarling dogs. He had no idea where he was being taken as he had never before been through this part of the camp, but he was mightily relieved when he arrived outside his own camp and was deposited among the friendly faces of his own hut.

For whatever reason, the SS had decided they had done enough to him. He was strapped up with an old khaki shirt by an orderly and put to bed. The release of anxiety swept over him and despite the pain in his chest, back and limbs and the intolerable pounding in his head, he knew he was very lucky to be alive.

He did not see Sergeant-Major Innes again. He was told he had been heavily involved with the Partizans since his arrival at Auschwitz and that fact had been revealed to the SS by an informer. Such was his condition, he was transferred back to Lamsdorf, but Arthur never found out if he pulled through.

CHAPTER 8

After just two days, Arthur was off the sick-list and back at work. The food rations did not improve and had, in fact, continued to worsen as the effect of Allied bombing cut deep into the German economy. However badly they fared, though, they knew they were much better off than their felloew prisoners in the Jewish sector. Frequently, British POWs would place scraps of food in a variety of hiding places for the Jews to take. This task was not shared by all. It was the view of more than one POW that it mattered little if a Jew died on a Tuesday or a Wednesday;they would die sooner or later anyway, so what was the point of prolonging their agony? The activity was also punishable with the kind of battering Arthur had suffered and many were not prepared to take the risk. It was a matter between a man and his conscience, but Arthur chose to do what he could.

He had made a friend of a Polish worker by the name of Maria Koska, who would feed him whatever news of the war she was able to pick up. It was from Maria that he learned the RAF were by the end of January 1944 bombing Berlin. She would pass the bulletins on scraps of paper and Arthur would later read them to his comrades eager for news. Maria was only nineteen, born and raised in Oswiecim and a proud Pole who hated the German invaders with an intense loathing.

Early that year, they heard the first of the bombers. From their reconnaisance, they had obviously learned of the industry in the area and had started to bomb sections of the camp, some way from where Arthur was. During the attacks, they would be moved to the air-raid shelters and Maria would sing for their entertainment. She had a beautiful voice and would sing romantic ballads of her homeland when they were free. She often sang with tears running down her cheeks and although Arthur could not translate the lyrics, there was no need. Their passion, warmth and beauty were all too apparent.

Other girls mingled with the British POWs and it was not unusual for romance to blossom. The degree to which this was permitted was entirely dependent on the attitude of the foreman and some decided to turn a blind eye. One soldier from Essex was known as 'Little Darkie' and was one of the few POWs at the camp who was younger than Arthur. He became attached to a

Ukranian girl named Natasha, a welder with striking good looks. Such was their mutual devotion to each other, they had decided they would marry and move to England together. They were, though, both tragically killed in seperate air raids towards the end of the war.

Arthur, too, was subject to the forces that push people together in such adverse circumstances and he and Maria would snatch together whatever moments they could. One of Maria's responsibilities was to furnish Arthur's gang with the flanges they required and she would deliberately give them insufficient for their needs to have reason to call on Arthur frequently. He, in turn, would keep a close eye on the level of the stock and was always the first to suggest their being replenished.

Sunday was generally a rest day and spent away from the overbearing misery constantly endured by their ill-fated Jewish neighbours. There were, though, irritants still to suffer and frequently they came from the French POWs walking Polish and Ukranian girls on the road outside the Monowitz wire. The British prisoners in the main had refused to sign a parole form that promised they would not attempt to escape if allowed unguarded outside the camp. The punishment for abuse of such a privelege was so severe that few used this form of parole as a means of escape. Some of the French prisoners had no problems signing the declaration and were thus rewarded with a greater degree of freedom. As they passed the British wire, they would taunt and tease the inmates, giving rise to a great deal of anger and frustration.

One Sunday, when standing close to the wire, Arthur and a few of his fellow comrades heard the sound of an approaching motor calvacade and were soon passed by a number of cars containing senior SS officers and, although he could hardly believe it, the head of the Gestapo himself, Heinrich Himmler. Arthur felt his blood chill as he watched the architect of the 'final solution' pass by.

The building work went on and Arthur was involved with a project of installing boilers which required the erection of scaffolding. A lad from the Royal Engineers known as 'Big Darky' had earned some respect in the camp for the brilliance with which he could move thirty-ton boilers around using only a winch and wooden rollers. With the assistance of only two sixty-year-old Polish labourers, they moved the boilers over ditches and around corners, patiently moving them, foot by foot, towards their objective. It was an amazing sight to behold. What made his presence all the more ironic was he had, before the war, been an employee of Babcock & Wilcox, so if his surroundings were unfamiliar to him, the boilers were most certainly not. With his quite brilliant mechanical mind, he became totally absorbed by the challenges set him and he seemed better able to cope with the horrific tapestry of life offered by Auschwitz.

Working alongside Arthur was a chirpy little Scouser by the name of Shaw, a former lorry driver for Pierrepoint. They got on well together and exchanged many stories about their experience and knowledge of HGVs. 'Big Darky' had ensured that the installing of the boilers had been completed without problem and Arthur and Shaw were employed to dismantle the 150 foot derrick erected for the purpose. They proceeded in a slow, methodical way to bring it down, but were constantly harried by the German foreman who saw their pedantic labours as a less than subtle form of timewasting. He cut corners, saved time and ignored warnings that the whole structure was in danger of coming down a lot quicker than he intended.

Almost inevitably, the derrick came crashing down, but did so with fatal consequences. The main part of the structure fell onto the roof of an electrics workshop and killed twenty Jews working inside almost instantly. The deaths mattered little to the hierarchy of both the SS and the directors of IG Farben & Company, but the loss of the premises was taken very seriously indeed.

Arthur and Shaw ran into what was left of the building to offer what comfort and assistance they could to the wounded, but there was little that could be done. No British soldiers were normally allowed into the workshop and Arthur could see why. It was a huge complex with rows of electric motors and a multitude of plinths onto which more electrical equipment was being lowered. This was probably the electrical nerve-centre for the entire camp.

The foreman was led away to be transferred, no doubt, to the Russian front. The SS showed no mercy to those who failed, even their own. A man who was guilty of working too feverishly in the cause of the German war effort was to be rewarded with a sentence that was almost the same as the death penalty.

As 1944 wore on, the British POWs became practically anaesthetized to the brutal treatment of the Jews. The officers of the SS seldom thought a Jew was worth the cost of a bullet, it being commomnplace to see the most severe beatings taking place or a man near death through exhaustion having the last remnants of life smashed out of him. A man would be kicked until the last twitches and nervous spasms stopped. Those witness to this daily horror had to each handle it in their own way, but they were all deeply traumatized to varying degrees. One man who arrived with dark, black hair saw it turn grey within a week.

There was no such thing as a good night's sleep. The noises of deeply troubled men crying and shouting out throughout the night made it difficult to put together more than a couple of hours of unconsciousness. Even when total exhaustion brought some temporary relief, it was usually accompanied by horrific, distorted nightmares.

'We don't sleep,' noted one rueful observer, 'we just take it in turns to keep everyone else awake. '

They might be woken at any time and tossed from their bunks. The cause might be a spot-search or, more frequently, entertainment for bored SS guards. It had the effect instead of maintaining a state of high tension.

Men could never could relax, tormented by their own thoughts and the menacing presence of sadistic guards. Many of them just went mad, snapped away from reality into a world even more dreadful than the one they had left. Some took to methanol as a form of suicide.

Each morning at five o'clock, the men would be woken by the macabre sound of the Jewish orchestra playing at the main entrance as the new arrivals were being sorted into two groups: those grouped to one side would be put to work, to the other side they would go straight to the gas chambers. At six o'clock, the door of the hut would be kicked open by one of the Wehrmacht guards amid the same routine of shouts and threats each day.

'Heraus! Scnell! Sie arbeiten schwer heute!' With the shouts would come the dreadful smell of the crematoria with which they lived every waking moment. There was no breakfast, just shouting, prodding and bullying in preparation for the six-thirty departure to the factory. The men were constantly weak and hungry, their bones protruding grotesquely through a thin, pale skin. Their heads ached almost permanently and their limbs were sore with beatings and malnutrition. Heavy with despair, there was precious little to live for. Arthur had no dreams of ever going home; they will not, he thought repeatedly, let us live to tell this tale.

On the short walk to the workplace, they would pass any number of Jewish corpses, beaten to death where they had fallen. They would witness many of the beatings, but knew now the price of interference was death. Once at work, they were never out of earshot of men and women screaming. It was a constant torment in the background.

Watching these people, Arthur became able to judge fairly accurately how much life was left in a man, although he was occasionally surprised at the determination of some who would cling on to life. The four-wheeled high-sided carts were pushed around the camp by two or three Jews who would stop to pick up the bodies of those recently shot or bludgeoned to death. It took two of them to pick up these skeletal frames as the men on the carts were only days away from death themselves.

The scene surrounding Arthur Dodd was one of constant horror, deprivation, misery and despair. As the winter of 1943/4 began to ease and spring approached, there was no comfort for Arthur. With the warmer weather would come disease and an increase in the stench of rotting flesh that was almost beyond human endurance. In private moments,he felt it was impossible to feel more thoroughly desperate, more utterly unhappy and more painfully miserable.

But it was a long way from being over.

Arthur Dodd

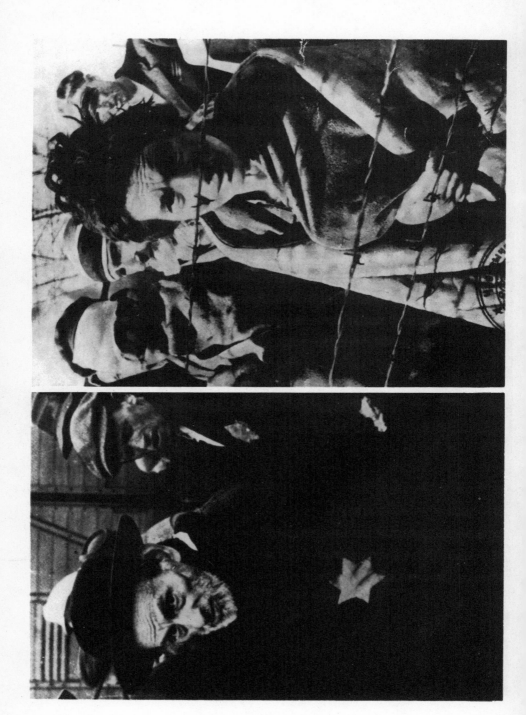

Auschwitz.

On the road to the baths, old woman with 3 little girls.

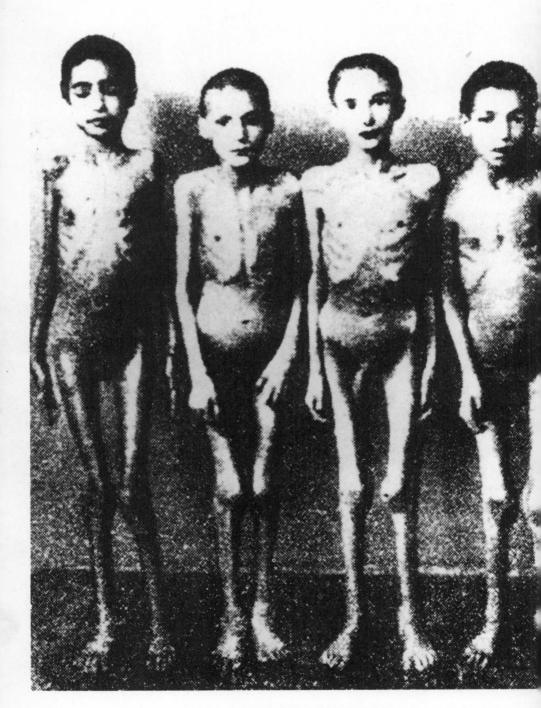

Child victims of Mengele.

Auschwitz.

Auschwitz.

CHAPTER 9

Slave labour was very much a part of the workforce at the Buna plant: Russians, Ukranians, German Communists, gypsies and, of course, Jews from all over Europe were pressed into service in the cause of the Third Reich. In the course of his own forced labour, Arthur saw men and women from a variety of nationalities and social backgrounds.

Arthur spent most of his time pipe-bending on a large wooden table with a metal worktop. Moveable steel pegs were secured in holes and traced the degree of bending required. Each pipe was filled with sand to avoid splitting. Once at their workplace, they would work all morning until twelve o'clock, at which time they would be fed on a serving of what was referred to as 'dishwater' soup. A twenty-gallon container was deemed sufficient to feed the several hundred people working in this part of BAU 38. The POWs were always fed first and what scraps remained were fed to the Jews.

The British POWs often got into arguments with the guards of both the Wehrmacht and the SS. They would frequently hurl abuse when a Jew was subjected to a beating and even if they had learned how far they could go, they did not let incidents of brutality pass without comment. Whenever the dissent became excessive, a guard would slip his revolver from his holster or raise his rifle and the objectors would generally stand down.

The working day would finish at five o'clock when they were returned to their respective huts. They were occasionally searched when entering the compound, as Arthur had been when carrying the wireless parts, but the men had no idea when it might happen. They might be stopped on three consecutive nights and then not be searched again for a fortnight. There was no way of knowing.

At half-past six, they would form a queue outside the hut to take their share of the bread and soup left for them. Jim Purdy would make sure the meagre rations were shared out fairly. Occasionally, perhaps once a fortnight, Jim would hand out the mail that had arrived and the men would form a separate queue in hope more than expectation of good news from home, but Arthur never received any post at Auschwitz.

Lights went out at precisely ten o'clock each night and Arthur would spend those hours he had to himself reading the King James bible he had picked up at Tobruk. The print was extremely small, but Arthur would study it carefully each evening, maintaining his faith and through it his spirit to carry on. Each of the prisoners was issued with one of the gospels from the New Testament, but few bothered to pray in such a God foresaken place. Arthur himself could not have coped without prayer and took his small bible with him everywhere in his field-dressing pocket.

When the weather was good, Arthur would step outside and stroll along the wire with the other lads. In this way, men from different huts met up and pieces of news and gossip were exchanged. There was also some banter about their respective areas of the country and their football teams. Light-hearted moments, though, were rare.

Sabotage was a thriving activity and the men would trade stories about what they had been up to. Filling pipes with rubble and loosening nuts after work had been inspected and passed was a regular trick. The men deliberately miscounted when mixing concrete and ensured the mix was too heavy with cement causing cracks in the structures that were built. One Polish electrician connected the mains to the water supply and they quickly disappeared. Another man obtained a whistle and caused umpteen delays in the working day by blowing it when he was out of sight. In these ways, the men did what they could to ensure what could go wrong, did go wrong.

The prisoners were constantly subject to abuse and tensions ran high. On one occasion, an SS guard burst into the technical lager (camp) and beat up a Jewish prisoner. After kicking and punching him repeatedly, he sent him sprawling into a British POW. The soldier snapped and stormed over to the guard and put a fist up to his face.

'You square-headed bastard!' he screamed, spitting in his face as he spoke. The guard went to draw his gun, but other lads standing by walked across and put themselves between the man and the guard. Anything could have happened, but finally the guard returned the gun to its holster and walked away.

Such incidents sometimes ended with a sickening fatality. A group of POWs marching to work passed a young girl struggling with a 'dixie' of soap. One of the lads took it from her to ease her burden, but was almost immediately tapped on the shoulder by an SS guard and told to pass it back. The soldier refused and stood his ground. Without hesitation, the guard ran him through with his bayonet and the man was dead before he hit the floor. It was never possible to know how far an SS guard could be pushed.

On another occasion, in the kitchens, a young Jewish boy picked up a piece of potato peel off the floor and ate it. He was spotted by a Polish woman, a falsche Deutsche, who knocked him to the floor. She then proceded to throw at him whatever came to hand and was only prevented from killing him where he lay by the intervention of a handful of British POWs.

Generally, the POWs would help when they could, but most of the time there was little they could do to intervene. One of the lads was approached by a young Jewish boy and asked for a 'piece' of a cigarette. When cheerfully told he was too young to smoke, the boy explained that it was for his father, who was a surgeon, and his older brother to share. When asked about his excellent command of the English language, the soldier was told that before the war the boy would spend six months of the year in Cromer, near Great Yarmouth. The soldier gave him his last full cigarette.

Two POWs once went into the factory kitchens to collect soup and bribed one of the kitchen hands to insert a figure '1' before the '25' rations written on the order sheet. The ten Jews working alongside them that day devoured the surplus rations. A POW escaped a severe beating once by quickly mingling with other prisoners after a particular dodge had been uncovered. Later, he was passed a note by a young Ukranian girl who had admired his courage in initially standing up to the guards. He had the note translated.

'Be careful. Do not become a flower in Auschwitz. '

Near the entrance to the gas chambers, were enormous beds of flowers and it had become symbolic for many Jews to pick a flower and take it with them to their death. The story was well known in the camp and the girl's message was not lost on the man. On another poignant occasion, a truck full of Jewish women arrived. They had, from the picture of health they presented, only recently been arrested and the POWs attantion was drawn to them as they sang together in Yiddish with voices so beautiful barely a word was spoken by the men watching. They were beautiful and brave and Arthur had to fight back the tears. They had voices like angels, he thought, being driven to hell.

Despite the treatment being handed out by the guards, especially those in the SS, not all the Germans in the camp were the same. One particular Wehrmacht supervisor was respected by the POWs. He was older than most of the other guards and treated the men with the respect he felt they deserved as fellow soldiers. He was once leaving the camp to go home to Cologne on leave and was presented with a package by the men. Knowing how hard times were for ordinary Germans, they had presented him with two packets of cigarettes, two bars of chocolate and a block of soap. Aware of how much they needed these rations for themselves, the man was overcome and cried in front of them.

In the July of 1944, rumours were rife that someone had attempted to assassinate Adolf Hitler. At first, the stories suggested he might be dead, but before long the word went around that he was not even seriously injured. In the August, there was a new arrival at Auschwitz, but it was many years later before Arthur ever heard of her. In Amsterdam, the Frank family were arrested by the

Gestapo after spending two years in hiding in the attic of their home. Among those sent to the camp was Otto Frank's daughter, Ann. Her diary was to be a potent testimony against the anti-Semitic regime of Germany's fascists long after her death.

As the summer drew to a close, the Germans were on the back foot. The Normandy landings had given the Allies a vital foothold on the continent and Paris was recovered by the end of August. Arthur did not know it, but the beginning of the end had arrived.

CHAPTER 10

As the Christmas of 1944 approached, Taffy the Choir got to work on the vocal chords of his fellow prisoners and his exacting demands produced a splendid oral performance at the carol concert. Such moments heavily reminded Arthur of the Holy Trinity church back at home in Castle.

Sergeant-Major Innes, the commanding POW officer badly beaten by the SS and returned to Lamsdorf, was replaced by Sergeant-Major Charlie Coward from the Royal Artillery. He was a native of Edmonton, north London, and had been taken prisoner at Calais in 1940. A large number of POWs arrived with him and assuming control he called a meeting of hut leaders, which included Jim Purdy. Jim passed on to the lads Coward's sentiments that the men at the camp appeared to him to resemble zombies more than soldiers.

'Wait until he's been here a few days,' one said, 'and see what he has to say then.' The Commonwealth was well represented at the meeting with George Randall from Cape Town and Ted Cockerell from Australia. Coward's attitude was one of giving the appearance to the Germans that all was as it should be and yet to pursue a strategy of countinuous sabotage. Every opportunity to inhibit the German war machine should be taken.

The subject of stooges was brought up and a man from Durham by the name of Miller with the Green Howards was mentioned. Apparently, he had arrived alone at the camp from Lamsdorf three weeks earlier and had aroused suspicion. Coward ordered the men not to discuss anything in his presence and ordered the only two other Green Howards in the camp to keep a watch on him.

At this time, Coward was able to communicate with officers at Lamsdorf and he sent a message requesting details on Miller. In the meantime, the other two Green Howards casually questioned him on regimental details, such as officers names and troop movements and he seemed very reluctant to answer their questions. Finally, word came back that nobody by the name of Miller with the Green Howards had come from Lamsdorf to Auschwitz.

The following morning, a handful of men followed Miller into the latrines and killed him. He disappeared into the pit. It did not surprise anyone that no comment was made by the Germans about his sudden and permanent absence. It did, though, surprise some that the usually meticulous Germans had decided to place Miller in the Green Howards Regiment, one of the smallest and thus one of the easiest for them to check out.

Lance Corporal Reynolds was a gentle man from the Midlands who was popular with the other men. On one freezing morning, he was ordered by an arrogant Unteroffizier of the SS to climb a recently erected steel pylon without rubber boots, climbing kit and gloves. Reynolds refused on the reasonable grounds of safety, but as he walked away towards the other lads, the German officer drew his pistol. The lads shouted a warning, but as Reynolds turned he was shot in the chest and killed instantly.

Two days later, Coward led the entourage to a nearby cemetery where Reynolds was buried with a Union flag draped over his coffin and as much military honour as the men could muster. The occasion was one of quiet dignity and respect, but it was little consolation to the men that the SS officer was removed from the camp and not seen again. Arthur had been a good friend to the man and hoped with all his heart that the murderer was on his way to the eastern front.

About this time, Arthur was approached by the same Polish worker who had arranged for him to receive the wireless parts. He told Arthur that the local Partizans were in need of the assistance of a few British POWs who could be trusted. They knew from the wireless incident that Arthur was such a man. The feeling of trust, however, was not entirely mutual. Arthur still had the bitter taste in his mouth of the beating he had received and was not satisfied the Pole was not responsible.

On the other hand, Arthur did not expect to survive Auschwitz and he was always tempted by any chance given him to put one over his captors. He had heard of the activities of the Partizans, which included the regular assassination of German officers in the nearby town of Gleiwitzanddecidedhe would go along with him. A couple of days later, he met up with the Pole and told him he had decided to help.

About half-four that day, Arthur was alone in the factory checking some pipe bends when he was approached by his contact and taken to the far end of the building, the first time he had been in this area. There were a number of bays filled with ceramic filters and after checking nervously that they were not being watched, the Pole began to claw out a hole behind one of the smallest of the filters. Having done so, he told Arthur to climb in and wait for someone to collect him. This he did, but it was extremely cramped and uncomfortable.

Before long, Arthur heard the other prisoners leaving the factory and being assembled outside. He assumed the Pole would make sure the head count was okay. Inside the filter bay, Arthur was terrified and had no idea what he had let himself in for or what would happen next. He did not know if he might be given the opportunity to escape or even if he might have been lured into a trap.

After an hour, he could bear it no longer and worked his way out of the mountain of filters and stood alongside it in the now deserted factory. He could hear the sound of dogs barking in the distance, but little else.

He stood there for hours, not knowing what or for whom he was waiting. His nerves were getting the better of him when he heard a muffled cry from the shadows.

Frightened half to death, he was beckoned by a nod of the head to follow as a man left the factory. As they made their way across the open ground, they had to keep an eye on the sweeping searchlights and take cover as they came around. His escort was another Pole, but he spoke no English and told him with sign-language to stay tucked in behind him. They made their way under the wire of Monowitz at a point already prepared, then crossed over a road and some scrubland. After an hour, Arthur had no idea where he was, but felt certain they were well clear of the huge Auschwitz complex. Any sense of freedom, though, was crushed by fear and anxiety.

Coming across another road, they were met by an old wagon and climbing onto the back, he found himself to be only one of five British POWs broken out of the camp. There was a tall Guardsman he knew as Ginger, two Geordies and a Yorkshire lad. After a short journey in the wagon, they were dropped at a small copse and were approached by the local Partizan leader who introduced himself as Alex.

Alex was a huge, burly man, clad in a sheepskin jacket and a bobble hat. His English was poor, but he was the only one they could talk to as the other four Poles spoke no English at all. He explained to them that since the collapsing derrick had crashed into the electrical insatllation, they now knew of its importance. It was their intention to blow it up and Arthur and his four comrades were required to help carry the explosives to the camp.

They were given a lift part of the way back, but again had to walk the best part of an hour to complete the journey to Monowitz. They carried boxes of explosives, batteries, sticks of gellignite and rolls of wire. They then re-entered the camp the same way Arthur had left it. The five POWs watched as the Poles wired up the electrical installation and then helped them as they trailed the wire back to the fence. Once a safe distance away, the detonator was plunged.

The explosion was muffled, but they saw and heard enough to know that considerable damage had been done. Wasting no time, the ten men quickly distanced themselves from the camp, but Arthur felt a sense of elation he had not felt for some considerable time.

Back at the copse, Alex would not allow a fire to be lit for fear of giving away their position, so they had to eat raw meat. Arthur was only able to chew it for so long before spitting it out, but it was still the best thing he had tasted in an age. With the meat, they had white bread, wine and genuine local schnapps. The POWs talked among themselves, high on the adrenalin of the mission and their escape from the camp.

They were surprised and somewhat alarmed when Alex later announced that they would be going back to the camp the next night to lay more explosives at the electrical installation. Although it had been badly damaged, it had not been destroyed, but the five British lads thought such a mission was suicide and said so. They were convinced the camp would be swarming with guards as a consequence of their success.

They took what sleep they could and spent most of the next day laid up in the copse like frightened rabbits. The food was the same as the previous evening except in daylight it looked slightly less appealing. The Poles chatted in their own tongue, but Arthur and his mates were tense and quiet in fear of what the coming night would bring.

Alex was aware of their mood and knew, too, that now outside the camp they were keen to make good their escape and get well clear of the camp. When they approached him on the subject, he told them of the importance of completely destroying the installation, but that after the job was done, he would give them whatever help he could in getting away.

On their way back to the camp that night, laden again with wire and explosives, Arthur was convinced he would either be killed in the next few hours or captured and beaten to within an inch of his life. Very few words were spoken on the journey. As it turned out, the mission was as successful as the previous night and Arthur was astonished at there being no reception committee waiting for them. Once they were safely back at their make-shift camp, Arthur and the other lads once again brought up with Alex the matter of their escape. They were less than impressed with Alex's answer.

'Gentlemen, very rare I have ten good me to do work. We must do as much damage as we can. One more task. Then you go. I help you.' They had no choice but to follow his wishes. It would be pointless attempting the arduous journey before them without a great deal of assistance from the Partizans. They were also acutely aware that this was war, they were soldiers and Alex was fighting the same enemy, taking no less risk himself than he was asking them to take.

It was a frustrating time.

CHAPTER 11

On the third night, they were loaded up again and set off with their Polish comrades, who they now trusted implicitely. They were by this time familiar with the local terrain and before long Arthur realised they were heading back to Monowitz. He could not believe they were going to the installation for a third consecutive night. The men exchanged furtive glances, each thinking the same thing.

Once more, they scrambled under the wire, lay the charges and retired some distance away. Again they were unchallenged. Arthur had nothing but admiration for these Polish Partizans and accepted now that they knew exactly what they were doing. By the time time they left Monowitz that night, they had not only destroyed what was left of the installation, they had also effectively sabotaged the preparations the Germans had made in the past forty-eight hours to rebuild it. The site was so badly damaged, it would be difficult to build anything there for some time.

On their return, Alex again told them that they must do 'one more job', but there were strong indications this time that he meant it. He handed one of the Geordies a rough map of the area, pointing out certain landmarks.

'You will escape tomorrow,' he told them.

'We can't be going to the installation again,' Arthur said, 'there's nothing left of it. 'Alex smiled.

'No, we are finished there.' The five former POWs were prepared to believe him. On the fourth day, there was added tension with the realisation that they would be on their way within a few hours. There being no light of an evening, Arthur had changed his routine and read his bible during the day. He found it difficult, though, to concentrate. He prayed for peace and an end to the war and he prayed for the tormented Jewish people inside the camp but his adrenalin was running high and it was difficult for him to think of much else but their forthcoming bid for freedom.

Before they left the camp, Alex embraced each of them in turn and shook their hands. What he said reassured them that he was as good as his word.

'We will not see each other again after this night,' he said, 'and we may not have chance to say farewell later. Thank you for what you do for my country. Good luck.' Even the Poles who were travelling with them that night shook hands with them. There may not have been an opportunity later. They were unable to understand each other's words, but translation was unnecessary.

They left the copse and travelled back towards Auschwitz, but this time moving further to the east of Monowitz. The British lads were not sorry to see this, believing they had well and truly exhausted their good fortune in that particular direction. As they neared the camp, it was clear they were approaching one of the Jewish sectors and Arthur was reminded of a rumour he had heard some time earlier of a planned mass breakout. Perhaps their mission this night was to coincide with that. This possibility was reinforced by the equipment they took with them. There were no explosives. Indeed, the British members of the party were not required to carry anything, but among the tools carried by the Poles were, Arthur suspected, wirecutters. As they approached the camp, it was eerily quiet except for the sound of barking dogs in the distance.

Then, suddenly, when they were still some hundred yards from the wire, powerful searchlights were switched on, blinding the men and lighting up the area as if it were mid-afternoon. Within seconds, a blanket of machine-gun and rifle fire opened up on them. After being momentarily stunned, they ran for cover as quickly as their terrified legs would carry them. Arthur expected at any second to feel the piercing pain of being shot in the back. Alongside him were the two Geordies. As they ran they each in turn stumbled and fell before scrambling back to their feet and carrying on. Arthur felt again his life was about to end, but this time there were no images of home and loved ones. Without any thought for his injured foot, he ran for his life as hard as he could. Dr Booth would have been impressed.

After a couple of minutes, the machine-gun fire receded behind them and they fell to the ground exhausted, barely able to breath. Arthur, with the two Geordies, had become seperated from the rest of the party and looking around in the darkness had no idea where they were. For a few minutes, the three men were totally unable to speak.

On reflection, they agreed that the gunfire had not been aimed at them. They were easy targets, but to their knowledge nobody had been hit. It seemed far more likely that the Germans had been informed of the break-out and switched on the lights as the Jewish prisoners were to meet up with the Partizans. In the bedlam that followed, they had been able to escape and had possibly not even been seen.

They waited for the Poles, Ginger and the Yorkshire lad to appear and they searched their immediate area carefully. They could find no sign of them. They were on their own. Arthur thought through what had happened on the previous nights and it was obvious that the plan to destroy the electrical installation was part of a plan to reduce the amount of lighting available to the Germans at the time of the break-out. In this, they had failed. The Germans had either utilized an installation in another part of the camp or had not been dependent on it for security lighting in the first place.

Although Arthur was not aware of it, the events at the camp that night marked the only occasion when a considerable number of Jewish prisoners reacted against the regime at Auschwitz. Some 860 Jews, generally those with professional skills, were put to work in the area of the gas chambers and the crematoria. Collectively known as a Sonderkommando ('Special Command'), their duties included the gruesome task of disposing of the bodies of fellow Jews. It was the most degrading and awful work that took place in the camp, but for the short time they were allocated to it, they were given some degree of preferential treatment. They were generally not badly beaten and their rations were sufficient to sustain them.

After four months, to reduce the risk of what was going on at Auschwitz ever reaching the outside world, the entire Sonderkommando was exterminated and replaced. Many observers have noted how little the Jews resisted the oppression of the Nazi regime, but this particular group of men decided they would not go quietly to the ovens. Using weapons provided by the local Partizans, they planned to shoot their way out of the camp. In this they failed miserably, but not before seventy officers or guards of the SS had been killed. Not one member of that Sonderkommando survived the day, but they did at least to to their deaths with their dignity restored.

The three decided to set off, but they had no idea where they were and so no idea which way to go. They had the rough map given to one of the Geordies by Alex, but it was impossible to fix on any landmarks in the dark. Their priority, though, was to distance themselves from the camp and they put several miles behind them by dawn. As day broke, they slipped into a roadside ditch and discussed what they should do next. They decided they would walk of a night and rest up during the day. Their next problem was hunger and they thought the only realistic prospect of finding food was to forage in the smallholdings of local farms and look for vegetables.

They made good progress on the second night and in the morning found what they thought at first were turnips, but were in fact mangols, a chewy, tasteless vegetable used for cattle fodder. It tasted like straw and proved to be totally inedible. To make matters worse, the heavens opened and it rained non-stop for the next two days. They were soaked through, cold, hungry and thoroughly miserable. They had discussed the possibility of knocking on a cottage door, but the fear of being reported prevented them. The taller of the two Geordies spoke a little German and was generally optimistic about their chances, making light of what they were up against whenever it was possible. His mate, who Arthur had seen more of at the camp, was the opposite. He was all doom and gloom and was convinced every hour was their last before being recaptured. Arthur quickly tired of his moaning.

Their plan to keep out of sight during the day worked well; they never once saw sight nor sound of anybody. After a few days of little if anything to eat, Arthur was as down-hearted as he could remember being. One morning, they stood on the brow of a hill and looked down on the valley below. To the left was a small village. They decided that they had no choice but to go into the village and give themselves up. If it meant they would be returned to Auschwitz they would have to accept it. The alternative was to starve to death.

They had passed road signs indicating they were now in Czechoslovakia, but had no idea of the name of the village. It was, however, very small and in the middle of nowhere. They thought it unlikely there would be a German presence. They made their way along a path which led through a gate and onto a road. They were close to the first of the buildings when they were confronted by a policeman carrying a gun. When challenged, the tall Geordie answered in German that they were Czech refugees. The officer then asked a barrage of questions in his native tongue to which

Geordie, smiling by this time, was totally unable to respond.

The officer led them to the village hall where they admitted to being escaping British POWs from Auschwitz. The officer then immediately called the German authorities, but had the decency to see the men were well fed and given the facilities to wash. They were treated with respect and the officer escorted them around the village for exercise. They were given a pack of cards, a dartboard and a small billiard table for their entertainment and the food was better than anything they had tasted since they left home. Their accommodation, too, was more than satisfactory.

They told the policeman about the treatment being handed out to the Jews at Auschwitz: the slave labour, the brutality the absence of food and, of course, the gas chambers and the murders. The officer nodded his head grimly. They told him nothing it seemed he did not already know.

They had expected to be picked up within a few hours, but by the end of the day there was still no sign of the Germans. They bedded down for the night and waited again the next day. Once again, they were well fed and well treated, and although they were objects of curiosity for the local villagers, they were met with nothing but hospitality and additional gifts of food.

There was no news from the German authorities and the days passed. The fact that they would sooner or later be returned to Auschwitz played heavily on their nerves, but they made the most of the kindness they received from the folk of the Czech village.

As it happened, two full weeks passed before the Germans arrived.

CHAPTER 12

It was an emotional departure from the village. They had no idea what awaited them back at the camp, but they feared the worse. The journey took the best part of two days and they were mostly quiet for the entire journey. Adding to their fears was the thought that they might be considered collaborators in the attempted break-out from the Jewish camp and suffer accordingly.

Arriving back at Monowitz, they climbed from the lorry and shook each other's hand, fully expecting that this would be the last time they would see each other. They were, though, left at the gate and told to return to their huts and await further orders. This surprised them. Arthur was in a different hut from the two Geordies and walking back alone he did not know what was happening.

There was only one other man in the hut as he entered and he hardly raised an eyelid at his appearance.

'How did it go then?' he asked casually. This was no way to greet a man who had been on the run and recaptured. Arthur's mind was racing.

'Oh, all right,' he answered cautiously. It suddenly dawned on Arthur that nobody was aware that they had, in fact, escaped. Why? There could be only one reason and Arthur went to leave the hut, knowing that he had to warn his Geordie friends before they let the cat out of the bag. He didn't get as far as the door when one of them came rushing in.

'Arthur,' he said, quietly but urgently, 'keep your mouth shut! Everybody thinks we've been on a working party!'

'I know,' Arthur replied, 'it can only mean one thing. It's a Wehrmacht cover-up. If the SS get wind of the fact we escaped, we won't be the only ones in for the high jump. Some senior German officers will be in trouble, too. '

'You're right! They're going to pretend nothing's happened!' After all they had been through since being recaptured, they could barely contain themselves at their good fortune. It had never crossed Arthur's mind that he might step down from the lorry and walk straight back to the hut as if nothing had happened.

Charlie Coward had a very different style to his predecessor Innes. Innes would not allow them to work in the railway sidings at the Buna plant, it being deemed as a direct contravention of the Geneva Convention. Coward, however, was only too happy for the men to work there, seeing it as an excellent opportunity for sabotage: stones and sand found their way into axle boxes, holes appeared in carriage roofs, damaging important equipment, and destination plates were swopped so that vital supplies for the eastern front ended up in Holland, while hundreds of tins of paint were sent to the Russian front.

More and more, they saw American Flying Fortress aircraft passing overhead on bombing raids. Each time, the air-raid siren would sound and the managers of the factories and the guards would run for the shelters, often allowing the POWs to make their own mind up whether or not they followed them. On one occasion, the siren came as an IG Farben engineer arrived at the camp on his BMW motorbike, which he rolled on its side and left as he ran for cover. The temptation was too much for Arthur. He cranked up the bike and rode it around the internal roads of the camp. When he put it back, he let down the tyres and put dirt in the petrol tank. As he returned to his mates, he was clapped and cheered all the way.

Up to that time, no bombs had been dropped on the camp, but the first time it happened was to Arthur the greatest living proof of divine intervention. The German engineer who owned the BMW called Arthur and five of his fellow POWs to one side and told them that the pipes they had installed were to be pressure tested. If the tests failed, they would be shot. The engineere was aware that the half-dozen men in front of him had been solely responsible for the job and the Germans were obviously tiring of the repeated attempts at sabotage. The men knew the game was up. The piping had not the remotest chance of passing the most insignificant of pressure tests. They had each filled them with an assortment of stones and dirt and Arthur himself had fitted two blank flanges.

The SS officer who Arthur had crossed on his first day at work had arrived on the scene and as far as Arthur was concerned , the game was up. Within minutes, he would be shot to death. Natasha came over to Little Darkie. She knew what they had been up to and realised that he too would soon be dead.

The engineers were preparing the test and as they did so, Arthur's heart beat like a piston as his life and loved ones once more came to mind. At St Valery and Bardiyah, his life had flashed before him as he thought he would die at any moment. Though the circumstances were very different, Arthur was this time sure that nothing could save them and the images from home once again came vividly to mind.

Suddenly, the air-raid siren sounded and the pressure test had to be delayed. It was but a short respite for the men. When the aircraft were gone, they would return to the factory and the test would be started. Everybody was ordered into the shelters. The fact that their shelter was totally inadequate for the purpose for which it was being used hardly seemed to matter to the six condemned men it contained. They talked nervously to each other and waited for the dreaded all clear.

Just at that moment they heard the unmistakable swishing sound of falling bombs, followed by a deafening explosion. Everybody was surprised by this turn of events. In every previous case, the aircraft had flown back from their raids empty. It could only be assumed that maybe the plane had only just been able to free its deadly load.

Whatever the cause, the plane passed and the all clear siren sounded. This usually welcome sound brought no relief to the men awaiting the pressure test. Arthur had, at the most, fifteen minutes left to live.

The doors to the shelter were opened and Arthur in his turn shuffled outside. The sight that greeted him took his breath away. One of the bombs had gone straight through the roof of BAU 38 at one end, blowing away the entire gable end. Dozens of distorted pipes swung freely in the air and smoke hung over the factory in a dark cloud. Looking around what he could see of the twenty-five square miles of Auschwitz, only one building had been hit and it was the one in which a fateful pressure test was about to take place. The six doomed men had to contain their joy, but their celebrations were loud and long once they were back in their huts.

CHAPTER 13

From that day forth, the Germans introduced a clever ruse to limit the damage of any air raids. Whenever the bombers were passing they released a dense fog from cylinders loaded onto the backs of trucks. These vehicles were parked in insignificant parts of the camp, but gave the impression they had something to hide. Bombs were then directed at these areas. As successful as it was, it was very much a case of closing the stable door after the horse had bolted as the BAU 38 building, one of the most important sites on the camp, was now destroyed forever.

There were a couple of illicit radios operating in the camp and by May 1944, it was becoming clear from the broadcasts that Germany was losing the war. This sparked an increase in the extermination of the Jewish prisoners, most of whom were Hungarian. As many as 65,000 would arrive at the camp in one day, with something in the region of 5,000 crammed onto one train of fifty carriages. Eight trains arrived each day, followed by another five every night.

In order to appease the new arrivals, they were led to believe they were being resettled in the area and some were even told they were being exchanged for German POWs via the Red Cross. Thus assured, they were led quietly to the gas chambers, only realising the deceit when it was too late. Arthur heard that such was the volume of the genocide that even an SS guard could bear it no longer. Working in close proximity to the gas chambers, he went out of his mind and was unceremoniously gassed himself

A new arrival was placed in Arthur's hut by the name of Evans who immediately began to arouse suspicion. He was both well spoken and well educated, but also remarkably well fed. His intelligence quickly earned him the nickname 'Professor'. He said that he had been an assistant pathologist in Canada to one of the country's leading surgeons, but the story was, like most tales in Auschwitz, treated with scepticism.

News of the war improved further as autumn approached and it was decided to hold a gala day.

Arthur joined up with Taffy's choir, the members of which approached their rehearsals with a dedication and enthusiasm normally reserved for the Llangollen Eistedfford. Reports of more Allied victories added to the buoyancy of the preparations and at times it was difficult to believe that they were amidst such death and perversion. On the day of the gala, there had been erected a coconut shy, a small roundabout,and a number of ingeneously constructed side shows. In the evening, a pantomime was to be held and the gala would have been a great success, but for the occurence of the greatest tragedy to strike the British POWs during their internment.

Early in the afternoon, as the men were enjoying themselves, they were interrupted by the air-raid sirens and as the camp was now being bombed on a regular basis, the men made their way to the brick built shelters, entered via a sloping ramp and closed off by steel doors. Arthur was with Spud Murphy, from Northwich, ready to close the doors once the men from the huts allocated to that shelter were inside. Just as the doors were shut, they heard an almighty swishing sound followed by a tremendous explosion. The ground shook and the far end of the shelter caved in as it took a direct hit.

Inside the shelter were some 150 POWs and nearly all were at least injured in some way. Arthur and Spud immediately opened the doors. Inside was thick with dust and Arthur heard a shout from the far end calling for any miners among the men. Both Spud and Arthur thought they had wet themselves, but closer examination showed it to be the blood from a multitude of tiny shrapnel wounds.

Within a few moments, a number of blond, blue-eyed members of the Hitler Youth arrived on the scene and worked as hard as anyone in the hours that followed to free those prisoners buried beneath the rubble. A medical officer called Harrison operated on a young lad with a hole in his head the size of a tennis ball. He left him holding a clamp to the wound.

'Leave that in, son,' he told him, 'it'll help.' Arthur helped another man carry the unfortunate lad outside and placed him onto a truck in which he and others badly injured were taken into hospital in Oswiecim. The rest of the day's events were cancelled and those still on the camp were left to mourn the loss of fifteen comrades. One of them was Big Darkie, the Royal Engineer from the Midlands, who had so impressed every body with his ability to move the boilers around. He was a great thinker and would have found the pyramids of Giza a fascination. He was a brilliant engineer and much admired. Another sad loss was Little Darkie from Essex, the lad in love with the Ukranian girl, Natasha. For her, his death was sheer heartbreak. He had been her one shining light, giving her hope for the future and a reason to carry on. She was totally crushed when the news was given to her.

Arthur passed one of the huts and thought he heard a moaning sound. This was the the hut where the pantomime would have been staged and on entering he saw some of the internal apex timbers had come down with the force of the explosion. Underneath was Billy Griffith from Birmingham. He had ignored the sirens to finish working on the pantomime preparations and had paid for it. Finding him trapped beneath the fallen timbers, Arthur leaned across to see if he was okay and was met with the broadest of cheeky grins. Even in adversity, this natural comic could raise a smile and make the best of things.

'Bloomin' heck, Brummie,' Arthur said, 'you don't look like you've got much to smile about. '

'Oh, I don't know, Arthur,' he replied, 'it's the first time I ever brought the house down!'

It was a day they had waited for with great anticipation and it had ended in tragedy. It was heartbreaking to think those fifteen men had endured all they had only to be killed by the bombs of their own side. Once he was alone, Arthur wept unashamedly.

It was at this time that Evans the pathologist's assistant had the opportunity to prove he was what he said he was and he did just that. Assisted by another man with medical experience by the name of Harrison, he worked tirelessly among the more badly injured men. The death toll would have been much higher but for the skill and determination of the pair of them and afterwards the men signed a scroll of appreciation which was presented to them both.

The dead men were laid out for each to pay his respects. Two days later a small service was held and the bodies were loaded onto a truck draped in the Union flag. They were taken to a small cemetery in the town and buried beside a wall in a communal grave. Fifteen POWs, one for each victim, were permitted to attend the burial. After the war, the bodies were moved to the military cemetery in Krakow.

At about half-past-ten every other Tuesday, the men would hear a train pulling out loaded with fuel for the eastern front. The Benzene plant in the far corner of the Buna complex, was already in full operation when Arthur arrived at the camp in the spring of 1943 and must have played a major part in the advance on Russia. One day, an RAF plane flew over and dropped leaflets warning the Germans to cease the train's movements. The following Tuesday, the British POWs waited with exitement to see if the warning would be heeded but the train left as usual.

The following night the bombers came and bombed the plant for a full hour. When the lads finally came from the shelters, the fires lit the night as if it were midday. Shortly afterwards, an RAF reconnaissance plane flew over and dipped its wings in salute of a successful mission. As the British contingent jumped up and down and cheered, they could clearly see the pilot raise his fist in determined acknowledgement. The men looked up to skies and Arthur was nudged by one of his fellow prisoners.

'Do you know what he's saying to us?'Arthur looked at him and shook his head. 'He's saying "hang on down there, boys, we won't be long coming for you now". ' The sight of a fellow countryman was an enormous lift to everyone, but like many men in the camp, Arthur still could not believe they would be allowed to live to tell the tale of what they had seen. As it happened, nobody came to liberate them. They had to make their own way home.

CHAPTER 14

Arthur was walking by the wire one evening after work when he saw a man limping past on the road running alongside the camp. As he got closer, he saw the man was a young German soldier returning from the Russian front. He looked no more than seventeen and had had his left foot blown off just above the ankle. The stub of his leg was swathed in filthy bandages and he hobbled along on improvised crutches made from tree branches. He was an ordinary young soldier, caught up in the madness of the times and Arthur could only feel great pity for him. It dismayed Arthur when the German guards did not even acknowledge him as he passed. He was never more certain that the Germans were staring down the barrel of defeat.

Slowly, more soldiers passed and they continued to do so over the next few days. Many had missing limbs, some were blind and being led by comrades. They dragged themselves along, their only objective to stay alive and make their way home to Germany.

The crematorias were busier than ever as the Christmas of 1944 approached and the stench of death was overpowering. Charlie Coward had been called back to Lamsdorf by its British camp leader, Sergeant-Major Sherrif, after the Germans finally caught on to his surreptitious methods. He was transferred to Teschen for his own safety and was not replaced. Coward's manner of dressing-up and socializing with the German officers was not appreciated by everyone and he earned himself the nickname of the 'Count of Auschwitz'. He did, though, have his own way of getting the job done and was quite prepared to push his luck to the limit.

The downturn in German fortunes was accompanied by an upsurge in SS brutality. Many Jews, obviously close to death, were forced to carry on with severe beatings. The behaviour of the kapos was all the more sickening, proving to what depths mankind can sink. They were only rewarded with their own single bunk and extra rations, but were prepared to torment and torture their fellow Jews and countrymen and women to get them.

There were exceptions. One kapo was a former American lawyer who had been trapped in Europe when visiting relatives at the beginning of the war. Arthur had befriended him over the previous few months after he had noticed subtle differences in his behaviour. When he was being observed by officers and guards of the SS, this kapo would rant and wave his stick with the worst of them, but Arthur noted that he would hit the ground or pull his blows as they landed. When he was not being watched he would cease his shouting and turn a blind eye to any bits of rations the soldiers passed to the Jews. He trod a fine and dangerous line, for his punishment would have been worse than death had he ever been caught. A short, thick set man, he was probably the only American POW in the camp, but his acting prowess was fit for a better stage and was to earn him life's ultimate oscar: survival and freedom.

One of the last of the British POWs to arrive was a 'Farmer Giles' character from Somerset. He returned to the hut one evening upset at the news that he had been taking part in the manufacture of submarine torpedoes, clearly a contravention of the Geneva Convention. The lads in the hut thought he was off his trolley, but he insisted he had seen the torpedoes racked up in a storage hut by the IG Farben complex. The following day, he was ecorted by senior managers of Farben and the SS to examine the contents of the hut in question. The men waited with apprehension, clearly expecting trouble. The 'torpedoes' turned out to be gas bottles and the men were never sure if the 'farmer' was as daft as he seemed or clever enough to dream up a ruse to disrupt the best part of a working day. In a consensus of opinion, few chose the latter.

Snow began to fall and more and more wounded German soldiers trudged past the camp. The soldiers of the Wehrmacht became increasingly disheartened and there was less supervision taking place in the factory. Arthur's weight had dropped from ten stone at the beginning of the war to six stone and food was as scarce as it had ever been. The situation was made the more critical by the complete absence by this time of Red Cross food parcels. They were restricted to just one diminishing piece of black bread and a ladle of soup given to them at noon each day. After that, they had nothing but an occasional cup of ersatz coffee.

Arthur was on his third reading of his bible from cover to cover and he was frequently abused for sticking so determinedly to his faith. Those who knew him better would leave him be when he was quietly reading, but others would taunt him.

'Where's your God now?' they would call to him, but Arthur ignored them. He knew that without his faith, he could not have endured the last couple of years. God, he believed, had been beside him every moment of his life. He noted that the same men who questioned the existance of his god were the same men who clenched their hands and thanked God for their deliverance after the shelter had been bombed.

Being some distance from the Jewish section, the British soldiers had never seen an arrival of Jewish prisoners, although if the wind blew towards them, they could hear the small orchestra that would play. One evening, they could hear some commotion outside and went out to see that the latest arrivals had been forced to leave the train early due to bomb damage of the line. There were some one thousand old men, women and children walking on the other side of the wire. The children were playing and singing and their mothers tried to smile for their sake. Once they were gone, the men returned to their hut in complete silence. They knew what the fate of those people would be. A Pole confirmed the following morning that every single one of those people, including the children, had been gassed during the night.

In the new year, news that the Russians were not very far away was rife in the camp. The men looked up the road on the far side of the wire almost as if they expected the Russians to appear at any moment. The SS guards were running around like demented lunatics and the POWs made a concerted effort to keep clear of them. Next came the first raid from Russian aircraft, dropping their devastating anti-personnel bombs for more than an hour. The shrapnel would scythe across the ground up to head height and instantly kill anyone in its path. They went on for three days, keeping the starving prisoners in the frozen shelter for hour after hour.

News came through that Krakow had been taken, which meant they were very close. This was followed with wild rumours that the SS were to destroy the camp and everyone in it. The first thing that happened, though, was a relief to everyone when on 15 January, a number of Jewish prisoners were moved west. This was the first positive indication that the SS did not intend a mass general slaughter of survivors before their departure.

As they left, they did not look able enough to walk more than a mile or two and given that they would be out all night in temperatures of eighteen below freezing without shelter, Arthur did not believe many, if any, of them would be alive the following morning. Those left behind were not convinced they would not be shot or blown up.

One morning, Maria came looking for him in the company of a Ukranian girl and beckoned for him to follow them to the eastern end of the complex. It was obvious that the men were not to be put to work on this morning, so Arthur followed. He was led to the upper floor of a building he had not been to before. Maria raised a finger to her lips and quietly the three peered through a window, but keeping themselves as much out of sight as was possible.

In the yard below, SS guards were shouting and whipping a number of Jews who were being forced to throw the carcases of dozens of their dead comrades into a large bonfire. The ground on which the fire was built had been hollowed out and so the bodies and materials were being thrown down onto the flames. Suddenly, Arthur was horrified to see small children being brought into the yard. He felt the bile rise in his throat as the children were kicked and booted onto the fire. Their screams were more than Arthur could bear. He turned away, his heart pounding in his chest. He believed that during the past two years he had been witness to every depravity of which man was capable, but now he shook violently at the scene before him Auschwitz was in its death throes, but in its final hours was able to produce a sickening horror beyond his comprehension and imagination. Arthur staggered back towards his hut, his mind racing, the screams of the children still ringing in his ears. For several hours, Arthur could not speak and it would be many years before he could describe to others what he had seen.

Sadly, he never saw Maria Koska again. In the madness of the time, it was difficult to keep a track of where anybody was and whether or not Maria survived is not known to Arthur to this day. Over the years, he has thought of her many times. He had a genuine fondness for her and wonders if she was able to free herself from the insanity that enveloped the camp in the final days. He will never know.

Two crematoria were blown up as the sound of the Rusian artillery could be heard in the distance. The fires raged all over the camp as much of the evidence, including paperwork, of the atrocities was destroyed. It was also a very dangerous time as SS guards went on a demented binge of murder. The British POWs stayed out of the way and kept an eye on the movements of any

SS guards. Most of the civilian staff and workers had disappeared and the anxiety affected the more decent Wehrmacht guards who feared the arrival of the approaching Russian infantry.

The tension that night was almost unbearable. The men knew they were close to surviving the horrors they had been subjected to for the best part of two years, but they did not know what was to happen next. Their lives could be taken from them at any moment. In the middle of the night, the air raid sirens sounded and the men rushed from the huts to the shelters. Many left precious personal belongings behind, but they were never to see the inside of the huts again. They were pinned down in the shelters for three days by the Russian air force, the attacks coming thick and fast. Some lasted a full hour and some were only ten minutes apart. It was during these raids that the grieving Natasha, Little Darkie's sweetheart, was killed. Those who ventured a look into the compound during a lull, confirmed that the huts had all been destroyed. This was undoubtedly an attack that would come before the main assault.

CHAPTER 15

After the third day of bombardment, there was a prolonged period of quiet and finally German guards appeared and told them to collect what gear they had and parade by the main gate. It was 23rd January 1945.

Basically, the men had what they stood up in, most of their property having been destroyed. For Arthur, this meant he had no balaclava or gloves. On reaching the gates, they found them wide open with about ten guards standing about. The last Jewish roll call had taken place some six days earlier and had been removed from the camp. It was still five-thirty in the morning but in the darkness they could see the damage caused by the bombers.

Snow was thick on the ground and the sound of the Russian artillery and infantry seemed so close he expected the lead tanks to appear at any moment. Arthur looked around at the bedraggled appearance of his emaciated comrades and doubted the ability of many to survive in the sub-zero temperatures. Arthur was dressed in full uniform and a greatcoat, but the size eight shoes he normally wore had fallen from his feet and he had managed to procure a pair of size elevens in the shelter. He had no socks and instead his feet were wrapped in a strips of an.old shirt, helping his feet to fit his newly acquired footwear. The fact that his feet were given so much space was a comfort.

There were some 230 Allied POWs and finally, as they pondered on what was happening, they were approached by the senior Wehrmacht officer, Feldwebel Messer. They listened to his words with a great deal of apprehension.

He told the men assembled that they were free to leave the camp; they were no longer prisoners of war. They could, he advised, march to the west towards the British and American forces, in which case, they would be accompanied by the soldiers of the Wehrmacht who would surrender. Or they could walk the short distance to the east where before long they would be met by the advancing Russians.

For Arthur, his mind was made up in no time at all. He did not fancy his chances with the Russians. They had no idea what kind of reception they would be given and had heard tales of the Russians dealing with all POWs as potential spies. He decide he would face the long walk towards the advancing British and American lines. If nothing else, he would be, God willing, nearer home with every step he took.

All but four Scottish lads took the road west and a story came back later that they were mown down by Russian tanks as they stepped in front of them waving their arms. The Russians were under direct orders from the Kremlin to get to Berlin first and anybody in their way was brushed aside. The story was never confirmed, but he never heard from any of the four again. Arthur was to later discover the Russians did not arrive in Auschwitz for another four days.

As the men set out, they did not know how far they would have to walk, but nobody was under any illusions that it would be less than several hundred miles. Arthur set off in a group with corporals Jim Purdy and Cummins, taking it in turns to look after Alan Blades, who was in a sorry state. They took an abandoned cart from the camp and pushed it through the snow.

With nothing to eat, they covered some ten miles on the first day and spent the night in a barn. There was, apparently, a German Hauptman travelling in front trying to arrange what accommodation he could for the men behind. Temperatures dropped to 22 degrees below in what was Poland's coldest winter for many years. They began walking the following morning at about four o'clock and had to walk over hundreds of dead Jews strewn across the road, partially covered in snow. Some had died of the cold, but others had clearly been shot in the head.

The column of men rested for ten minutes in each hour, but Arthur would have preferred to carry on, finding it very difficult to restart each time. In the course of the next twenty hours, they would cover nearly forty miles. Most of the men were beginning to suffer from frostbite of the fingers, toes and ears and some gave up the march, collapsing to the side of the road to die. There was a man known to Arthur simply as Sergeant Andy, who walked up and down the line to encourage the men to carry on. He would tell them that there was food and warm shelter waiting for them at their daily destination. Sometimes his resolve wore thin on the men struggling in the line, but as the Germans were determined to put as many miles between themselves and the Russians, his constant cajoling kept many men alive.

Arthur was free of frostbite, but every time he closed his eyes his eyelids froze and he had to rub them vigorously to get them open. At the end of the second day, they turned off the main road and walked up a tree-lined avenue. To one side was a large guest house and they were received by a stiff, little man who plied them with hot soup, bread and Ersatz coffee. Such was the relief at the warmth of the food, Arthur was close to tears.

Arthur was somewhat surprised he had not suffered from frostbite, for when it was his turn to push the cart he had no protective gloves. He had, though, befriended a man who was suffering badly with both feet. Arthur stayed up with him all night as he wept with the pain, but by the following morning it was obvious he could not continue. Their host promised he would be taken to hospital.

After the exertions of the previous day, they did not resume the march until noon and no longer came across the bodies of dead Jews, the SS by this time having taken a different route. They marched for just a few hours and yet still an increasing number were forced to drop out or fall behind. Arthur took a position at the back of the column but they were repeatedly stopped by their efforts to pursuade comrades to continue. Those they left behind were unlikely to survive.

They stopped at a barn, but there was no food awaiting them. They hunted around and found what at first they thought were potatoes but turned out to be mangel-wurzels.

The following day began at five in the morning and though they knew they were in for a long day, the sun was clear and they were warmed by the sun still low in the sky. Some of the men attempted to sing, no doubt inspired by Sergeant Andy, but it did not last long. In his walking up and down the line, Andy was still walking three times further than anybody else. He had made so many unfulfilled promises of food, little attention was now paid to him or his references to the 'white ladies', but he carried on nonetheless.

The days passed and they reached Troppua and continued following the German guards, assuming they knew where they were going. Just outside the village they were attacked by a single Russian fighter plane and scattered in all directions. It transpired that the only ones injured were those who left the road and Arthur and his immediate company decided in future to drop to the floor where they were if they were attacked in such a fashion again.

They had been marching for three weeks when they were next attacked, this time by a number of Russian fighters. The colum again scattered and many, despite the waving of white cloths, were killed or badly wounded. This was a tragic end for those who had suffered so much and were so near to freedom. Although he had dropped to the floor straight away, the spray of bullets had missed Arthur by a few feet and caught instead a young Geordie with whom Arthur had been walking.

The dead had their identity discs removed and were left by the roadside for someone else to bury. The effect on the column of being straffed by the aircraft of those purporting to be on the same side was severe. They were sitting ducks in the face of such attacks and the loss of close friends hung heavy over the men as they trudged on their way.

The Russian planes never came back. It was assumed they had opened fire on seeing the column led by German guards, but had pulled away on realising that they were followed by Allied soldiers. Periodically, the column was stopped while those unable to continue were made comfortable at the side of the road and left. Their fate was out of their hands, but few if any would have lived for long.

One evening they came across a concrete building that had contained Russian POWs and was fitted with bunk beds and mattresses. Many of the weary men fell gratefully onto them, but Arthur held back. He sensed the bunks were alive with bugs and dreaded the discomfort they could cause on the rest of the march. Life in captivity had generated in Arthur an ability to detect the presence of those tiny tormentors. He tried to warn the others but generally his words went unheeded.

That night he shared a groundsheet outside the building with one of the German guards and in the morning his caution proved to be justified, many of the men suffering from swollen eyelids where they had been bitten. They ate something they called potato soup, but which contained nothing they could recognise. Afterwards, what remained of the column continued, minus two guards who had left during the night, no doubt believing they would make greater progress unhindered.

By this time, Andy's promises of food were usually met with a chorus of obscenities but around noon on that day, they came across a party of Czechoslovakian nuns, dressed in white, standing alongside a van. They were served with plates of beans, tea and coffee, and because the nuns had probably expected there to be more in the party than by now there was, Arthur and the other men were for the first time in two years able to eat as much as they could. The van was picked clean of all it contained and as if this was not joy enough, the nuns reassured them they would be waiting for them again further on their journey. Sergeant Andy was elevated to near saintly status and he was never verbally abused again.

Some of the men had eaten too much and their emaciated frames and shrunken bellies could not cope with this sudden feast. Many stopped to be sick at the side of the road. Guards and British soldiers continued to disappear, but no attempt was made to stop anybody. Participation on the march was entirely voluntary and those who fancied their chances alone were able to leave. Arthur decided that with so many desperate German units roaming the area, safety behind the guards was all important. We need them now, he thought, as much as they will need us when we reach our destination.

CHAPTER16

By the end of March 1945, they emerged from the forests and rural plainlands onto a major road leading to Prague. The weather was kinder and the availability of vegetables improved. Each night they would break into the hog enclosures and steal what potatoes and turnips they required. The handcart, which they had been so tempted to ditch so many times became a godsend.

The produce was boiled up and shared with the guards, men of the Wehrmacht, with whom they had shared as fellow men their plight over the previous eight weeks. On one occasion, they had no fuel to light a fire and with great reluctance Arthur donated his treasured bible to the meagre pile of fuel they had mustered. Watching the flames licking through the wafer-thin pages was akin to the cremation of a dear friend, but Arthur felt that God had blessed his action. His journey through hell was near its end and the bible had served its purpose, delivering him sound of mind and body.

They arrived in Prague and crossed Wenceslas Square, where they were met by people cheering and offering them food and drink. They were grateful for the food, knowing that the Czech capital had had a hard time of it during the Nazi occupation and the people had little to give away. Corporal Cummings was pushing the handcart when he was beckoned by an old lady holding a huge loaf of bread. The loaf was the size of a bin lid and Cummings sent Arthur to collect what must have been near worth its weight in gold in those hard times. The woman was dressed in a long black skirt and wore a small hat. Arthur thanked her from the bottom of his heart and the lady simply smiled and pushed him back towards his friends.

Moments later a shout went up.

'Look out, Arthur!' Before he could turn, he was hit violently from behind and knocked out. When he came round some considerable time later he was reassured to see the loaf was by his side on the cart. He was later told he had been hit by one of the German guards who had a short while earlier heard his family had been wiped out in an air raid of British bombers. The man had been Messer's personal clerk at the camp and Arthur consoled himself with the fact that he was probably the man who typed up the report that he had been on a working party when in fact he had escaped. Later that day, the man disappeared, no doubt to make his way more directly back home.

They left Prague walking alongside a railtrack running parallel to the road. Up ahead was a train, its wagons filled with military equipment. Suddenly, RAF planes screamed down on the train and it was blown to the sky. As they passed the wreckage, they saw the remains of the unmanned rockets that terrorised London in the last stages of the war. They talked about the raid for the best part of the day, the sight of the RAF helping them believe that they just might make it home after all.

They came to Marianske Lazne and as they entered the square they were confronted by a mountain of currency. The marks were piled high, unattended in the centre of the square. There were few people about and the one person who seemed to be in charge was a rounded, bubbly women in her late forties and dressed in a smart burgandy costume. She told them they had robbed the bank of these worthless marks and invited the men to help themselves before she put light to it.

For Arthur, this was nothing short of plunder and he would take no part in it, but those who did were to benefit after the war. Far from the marks being worthless, they were bought off the soldiers for considerable sums of money when they got back home.

For tobacco the men would dry the leaves of flowers in their pockets and roll them between any pieces of paper they could find for a cigarette. Arthur, who preferred his pipe, would experiment with different varieties of leaves, crushing them into the pipe bowl and making a mental note of which gave the most satisfying smoke. What little comfort such inhalation provided was always accompanied by streaming eyes.

They crossed the border into Germany and came across the beautiful town of Weiden, a place totally unspoiled by the ravages of a war that had destroyed so many parts of Europe. The local inhabitants came out of their little houses and gaped with curiosity at the motley crew that passed before them. They were friendly and, of more importance, generous, supplying the men with meat and bread. It was a surreal world they had entered, as if the war was just a distorted figment of their demented imaginations. The people emerged from the immaculate, serene houses, dressed in a style unfamiliar to the gaze and seeming to belong to another age.

They were escorted to what seemed to be the town hall and were served real coffee. Shortly afterwards, the town's Burgermeister took them to a room where laid out on long tressle tables was an assortment of weaponry and military equipment, including some binoculars of the finest quality. They were told arrangements had been made with the Americans to hand in all known weapons to one central collection point prior to the town being taken. In this way, further unnecessary bloodshed was avoided.

They stayed in the town for a couple of days. They were shown the large houses on the outskirts, some of which had been occupied by SS soldiers on leave where they were encouraged to sleep with local blue-eyed, blonde women of the area to help produce Germany's future. Despite evidence of Hitler's empire crumbling all around him, there were many beautiful German women in the town in the last stages of pregnancy, ready to produce the next generation of the Reich. They left the town and within two hours, unbelievably, they heard American bombers pass overhead and a minute later the sound of the beautiful town being bombed.

Over the next three days they marched a further forty-two miles and reached Regensberg, where they were divided and billeted in different smallholdings. Corporal Cummings and Arthur stayed together as they had for the whole journey and were put to work with others filling in craters around the rail station. Alan Blades was excused all duties and was left with the one remaining German soldier still with them in a barn.

Their diet over the next few days consisted mostly of potato, although Cummings one morning caught a chicken as it walked over his bed. Within minutes, it was plucked and boiled up for breakfast. Strictly speaking, the town was still occupied by the Germans, but the Americans were on the other side of the Danube and ready to take it. On the second full day they were there, an American officer arrived in a jeep driven by a GI. He told them that the US army would be in the town within a day or two, but in the meantime not to be lulled in to a false sense of security by the apparent serenity that surrounded them.

'Keep your heads down and don't light any fires,' he told them. 'This ain't no time to slip up. You guys have been through enough already, I guess.' They continued working on the craters, meeting more and more prisoners making their way back from other POW camps. That night, they saw a light aircraft passing overhead and then noticed a wisp of smoke coming from a building a short distance away. The plane was giving an exact location of the fire to the US artillery on the other side of the river and a few seconds later the target was hit by shellfire. For the sake of brewing up, some two dozen former POWs were killed that evening within twenty-four hours of being liberated.

There was another raid the following day, but this time evasive action was taken and nobody else was killed. They sat together that night, in the company of the one remaining German guard, and talked about the following day, a day most of them thought they would never see. They lay awake all night, too excited to sleep. The Americans would soon be with them. They would soon be free.

CHAPTER 17

It was six o'clock on, appropriately enough for Arthur, a Sunday morning when they heard it. So quietly at first and then unmistakably, came the squeeking, rumbling noise of approaching tanks. One by one, the men were roused and soon the whispers turned to shouts and the shouts to cheers.

'It's the Yanks, lads! It's the Yanks!'They rushed outside and into the road to greet their liberators. The Americans dropped from their tanks and trucks and the men embraced. 'K' rations were thrown amongst them, each labeled breakfast, lunch or dinner. There were pots of jam, bars of chocolate and packets of cigarettes. There was butter and biscuits and too much for the men to take in. Arthur and many of those alongside him wept without shame.

Arthur ate the food and let the feeling of freedom and safety wash over him. The exhileration of knowing he could for the first time for so long look forward to the rest of his life was almost too much. He had been close to death too many times to count and he fell to his knees in thanksgivings.

They were approached by the officer they had seen a couple of days earlier and told they would be taken to Straubing, an airport to the south of Regensberg, from where they would be airlifted to the west. Arthur volunteered to drive the tractor which transported the men on a trailer to the airport. The tractor was an old delapidated beast which Arthur had to fight every yard of the way, but he was happy to do what he could to get everybody safely to the airport. Some of the lads were in a sorry state and he doubted if they had long to live.

As the men waited, Arthur spoke to the American officer and asked that Alan Blades be given priority and the officer readily agreed. Dakotas landed with supplies and took the men out in turn, some flying first to Brussels and the more fortunate ones going straight back to England.

After four days, Arthur's turn came. He sat in the Dakota, twelve men to each side and they listened as each of the square plastic windows popped as the plane became pressurized. The relief Arthur felt at finally being on his way home disappeared as he looked out of the window and saw flames coming from the starboard wing. He anxiously asked one of the flight officers if he knew one of the engines was on fire, but the man was unconcerned.

'The skipper will soon have that out,' he said. Suddenly, the plane lost altitude as if it was dropping out of the sky and each of the former POWs froze in terror. Within seconds the plane levelled and the fire in the wing was out. More than one in the company made use of the paper bags that had been provided on boarding.

Arthur arrived in Brussels on 8th May 1945, VE Day. Making his way through the city, thousands of people were celebrating in the street. By pure chance, he bumped into Fred Robinson, an old school friend, and they made the most of the joyous occasion. After six years of fear, never knowing what tomorrow would bring or, indeed, if there would be a tommorow, it was wonderful to be among so many people of so many nationalities celebrating the first day of the future.

Arthur and Fred's celebrations were cut short when they were arrested by two MPs for being improperly dressed. The fact that they had been POWs for more than two years cut no ice and they spent the night in a cell. The matter was put right the following morning on production of their pay books and after receiving profuse apologies from the officer in charge they were driven out to the airport. They were met by the sight of a line of magnificent Lancaster bombers and it gladdened their hearts to be going home in such style.

They had taken off and were over the channel before Arthur was aware they were airborn. He got to a window and watched as they flew over the white cliffs of Dover, a sight that brought tears to his eyes. They landed at Guildford, in Surrey, and were met by the WVS with cups of hot tea and broad smiles. Arthur's heart was near to bursting and though he must have looked as if he was at death's door, inside he felt like a million dollars.

He left for home the following day, travelling by way of London and Crewe. All he could think of was home and how he would decorate his father's house. He had received no word from home for the best part of three years so he had no idea what to expect, but he was excited at the thought of once again seeing familiar places and faces.

They say that the last mile home is the longest and so it proved for Arthur. His legs could barely carry him the remaining yards to his home. It was a joyful sight as it came into view, but approaching it, Arthur had a sixth sense that all was not right. This was reinforced when he noticed that people watched him from curtains when he would have expected them to come to the door to greet him and welcome him home.

As he walked up the path, he could see the house had not changed one bit since he had left it early in the war, but he felt apprehensive as he knocked and waited for an answer. The woman who came to the door was a complete stranger to him. He looked at her, but said nothing.

'You're Arthur, aren't yer?' she barked.

'Yes,' he replied.

'Well, you're not wanted here!' she snapped back before slamming the door in his face. He had not expected flags and bunting, but neither was he prepared for this. His father, he knew, was in the house, but had not had the nerve to come and face him. After standing for a minute rooted to the spot, he turned away and walked back up the path without looking round, making his way to his sister-in-law Margaret's small cottage in the next street.

She gave him a welcome fit for a king and fussed around him until he was near smothered in her kindness. She told him his father had married a woman from Liverpool a year earlier and they had already had a child. It had seemed that his father had allowed himself to be dominated by the woman and had not stood up to her when she laid down her laws. Arthur, despite his faith, was bitter towards him.

He had four months leave to sort himself out, but he found it difficult to talk with anyone. He spent hours each day walking and thinking about what he had been through. He would sit on the banks of the Weaver deep in thought, tossing stones into the river. The close friends he had made who had died in the camp and others who had not made it on that 700 mile march to freedom were very much in his thoughts.

His optimum weight before the war had been ten and a half stones, but he tipped the scales at six stone ten when he got back. Within a few weeks he noticed a multitude of small sores breaking out on his legs. He recalled the MO at Auschwitz had warned him after the air raid shelter was bombed that he might have many shrapnel wounds in his legs that would surface in their own time.

As he was still the responsibilty of the army, his own doctor would not treat him, so he reported to the MO of the nearest unit which was at the field bakery at Blakemere, Sandiway. The doctor paid little attention to Arthur's problem and listed him as 'M & D', meaning 'medicine and duties' andgenerally regarded as a shorthand for 'swinging the lead'.

As Arthur left the surgery, he was stopped by an old woman washing the step who asked him what his trouble was. The potential magnitude of the question caused Arthur to break down and he poured his heart out to the woman. He told her much of what he had been through during the war and when he was done, she took charge. She went in to see the doctor and after what seemed an age, she returned and told him the doctor would see him again.

When he re-entered the surgery, the doctor apologised and said he had not known Arthur had been in a prison camp and subject to so much hardship. Arthur wondered where he thought he'd spent the war weighing less than seven stone, but he said nothing and was grateful for the attention. He was prescribed an oral tonic and a paste to rub into his legs, both of which proved extremely effective.

Understandably, Arthur found it difficult to stay in doors during those early weeks and when a local councillor wanted to invite him to a forum at the local cinema, it took him a while to track Arthur down. He had grave reservations about attending a question and answer talk, but with the words of Maria in his thoughts that he should tell as many as he could about what he had seen, he decided to go.

Also invited was a paratrooper who had been at Arnhem. The councillor, a Mr Hilditch, asked the two men questions in turn. The audience applauded as the two men entered the stage, but as each of the paratrooper's answers were met with cheers and more applause, Arthur's descriptions of the horrors he had endured were met with an embarrassed, stoney silence. When the talk was over, the audience crowded around the paratrooper, while Arthur left unnoticed by a side door. The night was an unmitigated disaster and he vowed he would not subject himself to such a trial again.

All of Arthur's possessions had been sold to a second-hand shop by his stepmother, but the most serious loss to Arthur was that of his fishing tackle. This was put right by Margaret's brother, Harold Cross, who supplied him with a new set of tackle and from fishing Arthur was able to extract some form of therapy.

While on leave, he received mail from the army asking how much he felt he should be recompensed for the labour he had done while a prisoner of war with both the Italians and the Germans. Arthur suspected some ulterior motive in the question and spent days wondering how much he should claim. He had not done any work while a captive of the Italians, but in the end put in a claim for £30 for the labour forced from him at Auschwitz. When a cheque for that amount was returned to him, he would not have given the matter another thought had he not come across a former Auschwitz inmate. His friend was astounded at Arthur's paltry claim; he himself had claimed close to a £1,000 and been paid out without question.

When his leave was over, Arthur was recalled to Brighton and from there was sent to Hastings. He spent two months at Hastings before being posted to Western Command nearer home at Chester. After two weeks he was sent to a German POW camp at Wolgerton near Nantwich. Finally, he was sent to Blakemere Hall, where he had his legs treated and it he was here he met Olwen, who was to become his wife. From Blakemere Hall, Arthur was demobbed and returned to 'Civvy Street'.

CHAPTER 18

During his time in Auschwitz, Arthur had heard stories of the London Jew who repeatedly took risks to make contact with the British POWs and a few years ago his identity was revealed to Arthur as Leon Greenmans, camp number 98288. He defied all the odds with respect to surviving Nazi captivity, spending no less than thirty months in the concentration camps, of which two years were in Auschwitz. He was desperately unlucky to have found himself there at all.

Born in November, 1910 in Artillery Lane, Whitechapel. London, he grew up in Holland where he trained to be a concert singer. His wife, Esther Van Dam, was born in Rotterdam, but they returned to England to marry in Stepney Green in 1935. They then went back to Holland, where their son, Barney, was born five years later. At the beginning of the war he was running an antiquarian book business and making regular trips to London.

The birth of his son was registered with the British Consulate in Rotterdam and it had been promised that the Greenmans would be collected and taken to England when the Germans entered Holland. It never happened. When the Germans overran the country in the May of 1940, they were left behind. He handed his British passport and papers to a friend for safekeeping, but when he later asked for them, he was told they had been destroyed for fear of being accused of collaborating with Jews. He then contacted the Swiss Consulate, but their request for new passports went unanswered. Because of Leon's Dutch grandfather, the family were registered as Dutch Jews by the police chief inspector responsible for aliens.

In October, 1942, they were arrested and sent to the Westerbork camp in northern Holland and by January, 1943 they were in Birkenau. Of the consignment of 750 Jews of both sexes and all ages, all but fifty were gassed immediately. Of the fifty put to work, Leon was one of only two who survived. At the time he was marched away, he saw his wife and son being taken away on a truck. When he later asked a kapo what had happened to them, he answered by pointing to the sky. He never saw either of them again.

For two months in Birkenau, he was engaged in a multitude of meaningless tasks, the objective being to break what little spirit they had left. He was once engaged in removing a mound of sand from one point to another by means of filling the pockets of prison uniform. They endured rigorous physical exercise in freezing conditions, always accompanied by repeated beatings.

He was transferred to Camp One and regarded himself as fortunate he was not one of those taken to the gas chambers instead. It was around the April of 1943 that he saw for the first time the uniforms of the British soldiers interned at the camp. He was keen to speak to those he regarded as his fellow countrymen as often as he could, but the practice was seriously discouraged and could only be done by bribing one of the kapos. He would ask the POWs for cigarettes, which he could make a trade for soup slops from the kitchens. This was a hazardous business, but played a major part in keeping Leon alive. In return for the cigarettes, he would sing for the soldiers who appreciated the talent of his trained voice. He would shout across to the men, keen to let them know he was English.

'Hello! I'm Leon! Leon the Londoner!'

Leon never gave up hope that his incarcaration would be finally seen to be a mistake and he was keen to maintain what contact he could with the POWs. He took great risks to do so and was once badly beaten by a kapo for it after being spotted by a guard of the SS. The food and accommodation for the Jews was deplorable beyond words and they quickly learned that 'arbeit macht frei' meant you worked yourself to death and then you were free.

Many Jews were medical guinea pigs at Auschwitz and Leon was no exception. For some, the operations were disfiguring and fatal. Some women had their vaginas cut away, men had their testicles removed. Leon was operated on by an SS doctor, Horst Schumann. During his operation, Leon was able to cry out in English.

'They are hurting me now!' he shouted. Whether or not it was his using English, Leon does not know, but Schumann ordered the test to be stopped. Nevertheless, he was urinating blood for weeks afterwards.

After his release, Leon learned that the papers confirming his British status had arrived at Westerbork only minutes after his departure. For the sake of less than an hour, he had lost his wife and son and suffered desperate inhumanities. On leaving the camp, he was marched to Gleiwitz with feet so swollen he could barely walk. On arrival at Buchenwald he was admitted to hospital. Only for his insisting he was suffering with nothing more than chilblains, the doctors there would have amputated his feet. He was in hospital until April, 1945 and never complained about his feet. He knew if the doctors inspected them he would lose them.

It was on April 11th that Buchenwald was liberated by the Americans and Leon was flown to Paris. At the hospital there he was told that one of his toes had turned gangrenous and had to be amputated, a small price to pay and Leon thanked God that the operation had not taken place while in captivity. In October he was re-united with his father and stepmother in Rotterdam and the following month he arrived in London. There he was met by his two brothers, recently demobbed from the British army.

Leon vowed that if ever he escaped with his life from Auschwitz, he would dedicate the rest of it to letting people know of the horror of the camps. This he has done. He now lectures on the holocaust all over the world, speaking out against fascism and racism, ensuring that younger generations know what happened. For this, Leon is subject to threats and abuse from neo-fascist organizations such as Combat 18, but he will not stop. He is as dedicated today in his fight against facsism as he was fifty years ago.

For his defiant enlightenment of today's youth, he was, in the 1998 New Year's honours list, presented with the Order of the British Empire.

CHAPTER 19

Arthur Dodd does not underestimate the good fortune he enjoyed in surviving the horrors of the Second World War. At St Valery, Tobruk and on many occasions in Auschwitz, he did not believe he would survive. That he did, he credits to the love and compassion of God. Certainly, without his faith he could not have endured the trials of a concentration camp and would not have found the will to live.

He is the first person to concede that the treatment of the British POWs, as dreadful as it was, was infinitely better than that of the Jewish prisoners. His nightmare was not so much what he himself endured, but rather the inhuman brutality he witnessed. All of his worst memories focus on what he had to watch, not to what he himself was subjected.

Three weeks before the end of the millenium, Arthur will be eighty years old. In the twighlight of his life, there is nothing he enjoys more than gardening, fishing and bowling. He watches the constant uniformity of the seasons and wonders at the contrast of just how uncertain life can be. During the war, he lost count of how many times he confronted death. How many people can say their life has flashed before them three times?

There are few gentiles who can testify to the barbarism of the concentration camps. The current argument of neo-fascists is that the Holocaust is a fiction or, at least, a gross exaggeration. Tell that to Arthur Dodd. He has no political axe to grind, no theological or genetic point to make. His story is simply an account of what he saw and it has taken him more than fifty years to tell it.

Even students of the Second World War are generally unaware that British POWs were held captive at Auschwitz and there are now only a small number of them left. It was not until 1992 that they were first approached by the media. An article in The Independent on Sunday by Zoe Heller was based on brief interviews with the three of the surviving British POWs, one of whom was Arthur. This represented the first time Arthur had publicly divulged many of his experiences at Auschwitz and he found Ms Heller's treatment of the subject both intelligent and sympathetic.

Film-maker Maurice Hatton became aware of the existance of British survivors of Auschwitz after reading Primo Levi's account of the camp in 'If This is a Man' and put together the documentary Satan at his Best, a title suggested by Arthur himself. Levi was a trained chemist and had worked at the same Buna synthetic rubber plant, financed by IG Farben & Co., as Arthur. The close proximity of a coal mine, three rivers and an endless supply of slave labour made the location of Oswiecim a sound investment for the chemical industrialists, but it is to the credit of both the POWs and the Partizans that not one ounce of synthetic rubber ever left the plant.

For more than three decades after the war, Arthur suffered badly from repititive nightmares, migraine and other stress related sickness. Many times, when his sleep was disturbed and peace would not come, he would pick up his bible for spiritual sustinence. Once, in 1981, he opened it at random and began reading Hebrews 10: 32.

'Don't ever forget those wonderful days when you first learned about Christ. Remember how you kept right on with the Lord, even though it meant terrible suffering. Sometimes you were laughed at and beaten, and sometimes you watched and sympathised with others suffering the same things. You suffered with those thrown into jail and you were actually joyful when all you owned was taken from you, knowing better things were awaiting you in heaven, things that would be yours forever. Do not let this happy trust in the Lord die away, no matter what happens. Remember your reward. '

It was, however, not the bible that proved to be the turning point for Arthur. Picking up a copy of Reader's Digest, he read an article by Jules Segal, a psychologist, who had treated the eighty American hostages held in Iran. Segal referred to a large number of second world war veterans who had experienced nightmares for many years after their return to the US and stated that the most successful form of therapy had been for the survivors to talk openly about the memories that haunted them.

As luck would have it, Arthur was due to attend a meeting of the Methodist Fellowship the following night and he called the organisor, Roger Jones, and asked if those assembled could stay on for an extra half-an-hour or so, as he had something he would like to talk about. The experience in the cinema years earlier had left Arthur far from convinced that such therapy could work, but he was determined to see it through.

There were a dozen people seated around Arthur as he nervously began to tell his story. He described the brutal treatment and the murders, the skeletal frames, the stench of the dead and the dying. He told them about the gas chambers and the smoke, and the names of the German companies prepared to profit from the Holocaust. He told them about the man who traded the socks Arthur had given him for food, the young girl beaten at the the side of the road, the children thrown onto roaring flames. He related how he had watched a group of young children being walked to the gas chambers and how, all these years later, he still cannot look at schoolchildren walking in crocodile formation without crying. Finally, after talking uninterrupted for nearly half-an-hour, he broke down and cried. Roger's wife, Glyniss, came over to him and put her arms around him. Roger brought the meeting to a close and after gathering himself together, Arthur went home. Mr Segal was right. From that night, Arthur's nightmares stopped.

Auschwitz is still the first thing he thinks of every morning and he has been and will be forever affected by it. But the awful nightmares and the punishing migraine attacks are behind him. Two other Northwich lads survived Auschwitz. Tommy Dingham and Terry 'Spud' Murphy. He saw little of Tommy in the camp, but they became firm friends after the war. As tough as he was, he found it increasingly difficult to cope with the memories. He did not take Arthur's advice to talk openly about Auschwitz and refused to co-operate with the Maurice Hatton film. After spending time in a mental institution, Tommy died on his own in a small bedsit in February, 1994. Only six mourners attended his funeral in St Helen's church in Northwich, Arthur among them, together with his son, Geoffrey. It was a sad and solemn occasion and he turned to Geoffrey, choked with emotion.

'He deserved better than this,' he said.

Arthur lost touch with 'Spud' Murphy on the march from Auschwitz and it was some time later before they discovered they were both Northwich lads and met up again. Spud was mentally tougher than most and came out of the camp probably as well as anyone. He was an excellent footballer and managed Barnton Football Club after the war. Sadly, he died of a heart attack in the early eighties.

Arthur Dodd has kept his sanity by reading his bible every day. He was also assisted immeasurably in his slow recovery by his wife Olwen, who presented him with a son and a daughter. They in turn have given him six grandchildren and they are the source of much of the joy in his life today.

Arthur will never forget Auschwitz. But the memory of it now comes to him only in waking moments when he thinks back to an extraordinary episode of his life. He will forever be able to recall the most minute detail of what happened in Polish Silesia, but the nightmares have stopped. Finally, after many years of torment, Arthur has found freedom and with it some peace.